YEAR OF THE HORSE
FETHERLING:
0773724958:GEN.   :91.04.11
Pnf $ 19.95 00239133

YEAR OF THE HORSE

YEAR OF THE HORSE

A JOURNEY THROUGH
RUSSIA & CHINA

DOUGLAS FETHERLING

Copyright © 1991 Douglas Fetherling

All rights reserved. No part of this publication may be reproduced or transmitted in any form or by any means, electronic or mechanical, including photocopy, recording, or any information storage and retrieval system, without permission in writing from the publisher.

First published in 1991 by
Stoddart Publishing Co. Limited
34 Lesmill Road
Toronto, Canada
M3B 2T6

Canadian Cataloguing in Publication Data

Fetherling, Douglas, 1949-
Year of the horse

ISBN 0-7737-2495-8

1. Fetherling, Douglas, 1949-   Journeys -   Soviet Union.
2. Fetherling, Douglas, 1949-   Journeys -   China.
3. Soviet Union -   Description and travel -   1970- .
4 . China -   Description and travel -   1976- .
I. Title

DK29.F48 199 1914.7'04854 C91-093423-1

Printed in The United States of America
Jacket Design: Linda Menyes

For John Fraser and Elizabeth MacCallum
(China hands)

CONTENTS

Preface   xi

One: False Starts   1
Two: On the Loose in Moscow   18
Three: Arts and Letters   42
Four: Red Arrow, Red Square   56
Five: Diseases of the Soul   75
Six: Transsib   84
Seven: Comparative Embalming   105
Eight: Chongqing!   115
Nine: Downriver   132
Ten: The Buzz on the Shanghai Bund   149
Eleven: Evil Person Gangs   165

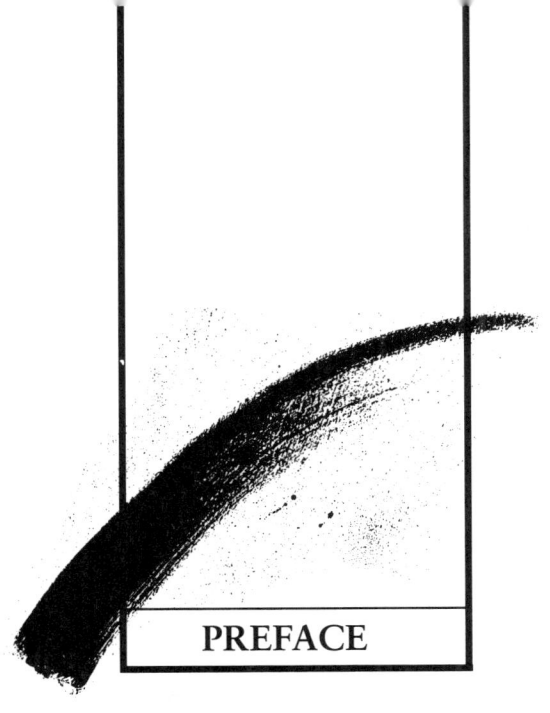

PREFACE

This is an account of a trip through Russia and China to Southeast Asia in the spring of 1990, when all those places, but especially the U.S.S.R., seemed to vibrate in the expectation that important events were underway or about to begin. The end of the Cold War and the dismantling of the Eastern Bloc (and of the Berlin Wall that symbolized it) came in tandem with what struck many people as an unstoppable counter-revolution in the Soviet Union. The situation there was the mirror image of that in China, where the pro-democracy movement had been suppressed so cruelly. Yet the two occurrences clearly were manifestations of the same urge, a demand for democracy in many regions of the world not lucky enough to have had recent experience of it.

The editor of my newspaper called this phenomenon "part of the major story of our time" and wished me to bring back an account of what I saw, with particular emphasis on any direct comparisons I could draw between everyday life in the Soviet Union and the People's Republic. The aim was far more modest than that makes it sound. I'm not a political analyst or economist but merely a gadfly, and the trip, like all such trips, took many unexpected twists and turns. What I strove to produce wasn't straight travel-writing. Nor was it reportage, though I tried to be accurate and informative and to think about what I had seen. What to call it then? "Diagnostic impressionism" is a ridiculous mouthful yet it does suggest what I was groping for. In any case, I was able for the most part to resist the pull of prophecy. But in those cases where I gave in to temptation and have been proved wrong—well, my defence is that I was only showing matters as they seemed at the time under discussion. As the atheist said when ascending to Heaven, "I was mistaken."

Most of the following pages were written in a notebook using my knees for a desk as I bounced along on trains or boats or lolled in lobbies and ante-rooms, sometimes under the gaze of people with automatic weapons. Their stares would cause me to bury my nose even deeper in my scribbling, which in turn intensified their curiosity—until they got bored, much to my relief, and wandered off to be suspicious of someone else. By that method of composition I was able to keep the narrative going, picking it up fresh each morning, not knowing where it would take me by nightfall. Later, over the course of several days in cafés and bars in Bangkok, I strung the episodes together. The manuscript was then published as an issue of *The Whig-Standard Magazine* following some editorial work by Roger Bainbridge and David Prosser, to whom my thanks. I then recast, expanded, and corrected the material for this book. I have updated it here and there, as seemed appropriate, but I have not attempted to extend my comments into the present. Given the speed with which

PREFACE

events in the Soviet Union (and other places) continue to move, that would be an impossible task and no doubt self-defeating. Tomorrow's details will eclipse today's. I've tried only to recapture the mood I experienced and to guess at the reasons for it.

Douglas Fetherling
December 1990

YEAR OF THE HORSE

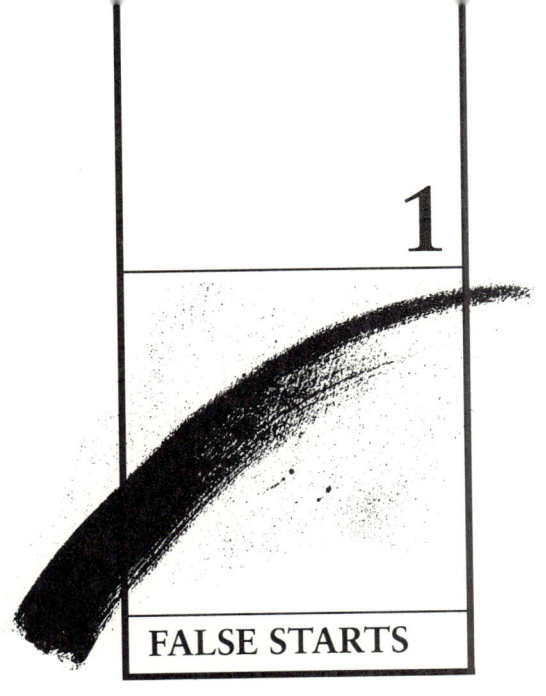

1

FALSE STARTS

I looked up from my work to find the room filling with Russians. Given that I was in Kingston, Ontario, labouring on *The Whig-Standard*, one might imagine that such an occurrence was sufficiently unexpected to justify some remark or exclamation. But the *Whig* is a most unusual newspaper, with ambitions far in excess of its modest circulation, and people employed there have come to accept that little anomalies of vision and behaviour sometimes punctuate their day. At least I had.

I was on the first floor, in the quarters of the editorial page, at a desk immediately outside the office of the paper's editor. I glanced up from the proof I was reading as a man in a dark blue suit stepped out of the small crowd and spoke to me, asking in a thick Russian accent for Neil Reynolds, the *Whig*'s laser-eyed editor. I pointed the visitor in the right direction and he disappeared inside, followed by his companions, walking in single file like a family of ducks. I thought no more about it.

The *Whig* is an old publication — it makes claim in fact to being Canada's oldest daily — and over many generations a complex and often emotional relationship has been built up between the institution and the community. Local causes, issues, crusades, and crises consume the attention of the staff and the citizenry to an extent sometimes difficult for outsiders to warrant or believe. This is somehow tied to the fact that the paper has been practically fetishistic about free speech, with the result that it seems to constantly reflect a din of opinion from both political extremes (often to the detriment of the area in the middle that most other Canadian newspapers call home).

On quite another plane, however, the *Whig* had sometimes been, over the past dozen or so years, a net exporter of news and opinion to the rest of the country. Under Michael Davies, the third of his clan to be publisher, and with Reynolds as editor, it had thrown enormous resources of time, space, and money into lengthy investigations of everything from alleged war criminals to the illegal traffic in endangered birds, winning no end of grief and a wall full of national awards. One of the most celebrated instances of its initiative was the occasion in 1986, during the Soviet occupation of Afghanistan, when the paper dispatched a journalist and two photographers into Soviet-occupied territory in order to publicize the plight of Red Army defectors held by the Afghan resistance.

The Soviets had some reason to harbour a dislike of the *Whig*'s editor, a person so consumed by politics that he has a satellite dish at his house in the country so he can watch a Soviet magazine show on television. Now, with Mikhail Gorbachev in power and *glasnost* completely supplanting the mere detente that used to pass for co-operation between

East and West, Reynolds had another idea. He would put to the test Soviet claims about the spirit of reform and their openness to new ideas, particularly ones that were old hat in the West.

Each country had resident correspondents in the other's capital, of course, but neither nation's media people really knew much about their opposite numbers, and so Reynolds quietly entered into negotiation with the Soviet embassy in Ottawa regarding a journalistic exchange programme. He proposed that *The Whig-Standard* send some people to work on Soviet newspapers and itself play host to some Soviet reporters, so that each could see the other's country from the perch, if not necessarily the perspective, of the local press. He must have reasoned that if the Soviets accepted, it would be absolute proof of their desire for co-operation.

They accepted. Which explained the hushed conference between Reynolds and various Soviet officials, a type of event that would become increasingly common.

I found out about all this only later, once I had already begun planning a fact-finding trip through China and Southeast Asia.

A year or two earlier, my friend Robert Fulford, momentarily at leisure after leaving the editorship of *Saturday Night*, went to Japan on a fellowship from the Asia Pacific Foundation of Canada, a body with the stated purpose of raising Canada's consciousness about the Pacific Rim. He urged me to apply for such a grant myself, and pledged his support. I am not, by nature or design, a competitor; motivated by artificial disdain masking a strong desire to avoid certain disappointment, I generally do not participate in any situation that resembles a beauty contest. But this time I made an exception. I had a longstanding interest in Chinese social history, though that term is far loftier than my low level of knowledge would justify. Also, as with many people my age, Vietnam had occupied much of my waking thoughts twenty-five years ago, when the American war was at its peak, but now I found myself with a revived fascination for the place. So I wanted to take a river trip down the Yangtze, or that part of it where the famous Three Gorges were being menaced by the possibility of a huge hydroelectric project that threatened to flood them one day. And I wanted to see first hand what ordinary existence was like in the Vietnamese cities now, a subject about which I was hearing and reading much scuttlebutt.

Bob Fulford would endorse my application for travel money, but I needed additional sponsors as well. I threw myself on the mercy of two other friends, Charles Taylor, the former foreign correspondent, and George Woodcock, the man of letters, who between them have published a whole shelf of books about Asia. When both graciously agreed to perjure themselves on the subject of my alleged abilities, I went ahead and applied to the foundation's jurors. And they accepted.

I began to get excited. All the more so after Neil Reynolds told me of his plans, hinting that I might like to be a part of the scheme. But as I have often found in the past, the adrenaline released by such grand hopes is often used up in battling the resultant frustration.

Neil Reynolds had worked out an ambitious programme for the *Whig*'s coverage of the changes inside the U.S.S.R. I would be stationed for a month at one of the newspapers or magazines in Moscow, writing articles for translation into Russian. All the while, I would scurry about interviewing officials, dissidents, citizens, underground artists, and so on, taking copious notes for use in what I would later contribute to the *Whig*. Meanwhile, Ann Lukits, one the *Whig*'s most able journalists, and her husband, Steve, who had recently joined the staff as an editorial writer, would go to Kiev with their new baby and try to live as ordinary Soviets do, queuing and bartering their way through daily life. At my urging, Neil was also going to send Greg Burliuk, the paper's rock critic, who had recently written a sensitive and powerful article for *The Whig-Standard Magazine* about his Ukrainian heritage. It was assumed that Jack Chiang, the picture editor and no doubt one of Canada's two or three most accomplished newspaper photographers, would go as well; his documentation had been a vital part of a number of the *Whig*'s editorial adventures, including the Afghanistan mission.

Significantly, or at least appropriately, my part of the collective reporting job would conclude just after May Day, the best-known celebration in the Soviet calendar. As I envisioned the itinerary, I would then board the Trans-Siberian Railway for the famously gruelling trip to Beijing, eight time zones and 9,000 kilometres distant. From there I wanted to strike southwestward, to Chongqing, some 2,500 hundred kilometres away, and embark down the middle section of the Yangtze, towards Shanghai, a city so vibrant and individualistic, it is said, that not even the Cultural Revolution had quite managed to extinguish its spark. Relations between the People's Republic and Vietnam had been improving of late, partly as a result of Vietnam's withdrawal from Cambodia. But it still was not possible to go directly from the one nation to the other by ordinary transport. So I would make my way to Bangkok and enter Vietnam from there, and travel between Hanoi and Ho Chi Minh City by rail, on the Reunification Express. Then I would push on to Hong Kong, which in so many ways seems the nerve centre of Asian politics at the moment, what with the influx of poor Vietnamese boat people and the corresponding out-migration of prosperous Hongkongese fearful of what will happen when Britain's lease on most of the colony expires in 1997.

One day I was in the office of Michael Davies, getting the benefit of his own experiences in China, when he sprang to his feet and began tracing the route with his finger on the enormous globe that stood in one corner of the room. The prospect suddenly seemed daunting for a hardened introvert like myself, but by that time I was wondering whether the trip would take place at all, for I was smack in the middle of assorted delays and misfortunes.

Of the places I was hoping to visit, Vietnam was the one with the reputation for being most hesitant about admitting ordinary travellers, much less journalists. A year or so earlier, there was a brief flurry of welcome, and many U.S. veterans, for example, were suffered to take conducted tours of the old battlefields and Viet Cong tunnels in return for their sorely needed hard currency, but the novelty soon wore off. The Vietnamese, however, were turning out to be the least suspicious and least bureaucratically minded of the nationalities I was dealing with. They charged US$100 for a visa, or more than five times what the Soviets demanded for one of theirs, but asked only a few perfunctory questions and didn't seem to care what my profession was. Their only stipulation — and it came as a blow — was that I not ride the trains, which after years of being off-limits had recently been opened up to westerners, or so I had been told. "Too dangerous for westerners now", they said. I remembered hearing some gossip in London the previous winter about how the pullback from Cambodia had created a surplus of Cambodian soldiers, more than Cambodia's internal struggles, bloody though they were, could absorb, and that some of these men had turned to banditry along the frontier — and no doubt across it as well. Was this the reason for condemning me to domestic air travel? I never found out, but I know now what I didn't know then: that Vietnam, after being open for a while, was closing down again in fear.

The next set-back came from within when the recession that most everyone had been expecting suddenly arrived at the *Whig*. At the time of which I speak, the paper was still a sole proprietorship, free to pursue goals and policies that are usually anathema to the newspaper chains (one of which, Southam Inc., has since gained control). That was one of the *Whig*'s most important strengths. But the negative side was that, with not so much as a radio or TV licence to share the strain of lean times, the paper was more sensitive to economic currents than most are. One result, perhaps, was a sort of budgetary bulimia. Now, suddenly, the crunch had come, bringing a hiring freeze and other restraints — and the cancellation of the Russian programme or most of it. I didn't know how disappointed Greg Burliuk and Jack Chiang were, but I sensed that the Lukitses, for their part, were secretly relieved: they had been worried, and rightly so, about moving their little one so near Chernobyl, the site of the world's worst nuclear accident only three years earlier. Since the Asia Pacific Foundation was paying for most of my trip, I was spared, in theory. Yet my funds were earmarked for Asian, not Slavic territory, and in any event could not be stretched to cover the high cost of a rather long stay in Moscow; I would have to be dependent on the hospitality of my Soviet hosts — and their offer of free room and board was about to collapse, since it was not clear whether the *Whig* would any longer be in a position to extend the same courtesy to my opposite number when he or she, or they, came to stay in Kingston. I managed to salvage the situation, at some cost to my nervous system, only by getting Moscow to agree to delay sending its party until the *Whig* had struggled through the current fiscal period.

My other problem was China.

Not long after I received the favourable news from the foundation, the whole complexion of the proposed trip changed when the troops rolled into Tiananmen Square in Beijing and massacred many hundreds, and probably thousands, of the students who were protesting peacefully enough for democracy (an event made all the more vivid for me by a *samizdat* audiotape that came my way, full of gunfire and screams). That was June 1989. My wife Janet had been intending to meet up with me in Shanghai, but now she decided not to go, saying repeatedly, "They're not getting a cent of mine." I fully shared her indignation but couldn't quite separate my professional obligations from my private feelings. Also, she had been to China before; I had not, and wished to avoid blowing my most obvious chance.

By their actions, the Chinese had become the outcasts of the diplomatic world, and though this condition obtained for only a very short time, before both the U.S. and Canada re-embraced them with unseemly haste though perhaps also with dubious sincerity, it coincided with the period in which I had to approach the Chinese authorities for help.

Whenever I pass an embassy or consulate (even Kingston has two — Dutch and Italian) my mind is always carried back to Australia and a walk through embassy row in Canberra. The foreign missions there are built in the architectural styles of the various countries, so that the U.S. embassy is a heavily armed imitation of a Southern plantation house, the Japanese one is a mock pagoda — and Canada's commission an appallingly perfect representation of Toronto urban sprawl, say, Bathurst Street at Wilson Avenue, circa 1968. In Ottawa the situation is quite different, a hymn to what architectural historians call adaptive reuse. The Cuban embassy, for example, occupies a mammoth Victorian house of the sort that, in small Ontario towns, has invariably been made into a funeral home. The Chinese embassy is an enormous square pile of limestone, grey within and without. It was formerly a convent.

As the *Whig*'s literary editor (a sort of secular prebendary), I suppose I could have gone there to obtain an ordinary tourist visa, for I am not a reporter in any generally accepted sense of the term. Such would have given me more freedom in one sense, for I would have been less conspicuous, but would have been confining in another, since I would have been prohibited from interviewing and enquiring if the mood or opportunity allowed. I saw no reason to be other than straightforward and so arrived at the embassy to have my journalistic credentials, such as they are, examined by one of the first secretaries (in the Chinese foreign service, most everyone is a first secretary, in somewhat the same way that all FBI agents are known as special agents). He came striding confidently into the reception area with his right hand extended and led me through a maze of interior spaces to a large high-ceilinged room at the back, an old classroom perhaps, or maybe a dormitory. It was bare except for a sofa and a low table at the far end; a half-metre-high thermos of tea stood on the floor near the sofa. My host bade me to sit and we began to chat. His second question was, "How did your newspaper cover the June uprising in Beijing?"

This was franker than I had expected him to be, and I tried to repay his candour in kind without damaging my position. I allowed that, yes, in the immediate aftermath of the event, someone — someone other than myself, though this was a matter of caprice rather than design — wrote a long editorial denouncing the Chinese government, but that the actual news coverage was drawn of course from the wire services. I didn't know how much the first secretary knew about the Canadian news media — enough, it sometimes seemed — but I ventured to observe that Canadian television stations have access to reports from the Beijing correspondents of the Canadian networks, but that the daily newspapers, other than *The Globe and Mail*, the *Toronto Star* and some others, were forced to rely more heavily on foreign wire services, particularly American ones, and that therefore the stories tend to reflect American preconceptions. Wasn't this all the more reason, I suggested, for an independent Canadian paper like the *Whig* to send an observer so that he could relay what he saw to its readers in some approximation of their own voice? I could be mistaken, but I thought that my interlocutor betrayed just the faintest trace of a smile at how the Ping Pong ball had been returned to his side of the table. The game lasted another twenty minutes or so. At its conclusion, I was advised to write to the All-China Journalists' Association in Beijing and beg an invitation, without which I could not get a visa. In a couple of days' time, I had completed the task.

While I was laying these plans, I was also, like the rest of the world, watching, transfixed, as the pace of political change inside Eastern Europe and the Soviet Union gained momentum. Centrifugal force was having a wild holiday, as first Azerbaijan and then Lithuania asserted their independent spirit, with Gorbachev giving them and other republics more slack but also warning them not to use it. It was clear that he viewed the breaking away of East Germany, Poland, and Hungary much more favourably than he did similar urges within the Soviet federation. Here was the paradox: while he was assuming greater and greater power himself, he was also distributing power more freely to others. It was by that means, clearly, that he hoped to stem the dissatisfaction of the citizenry. And yet the people, it seemed, were getting fed up with change for its own sake, as distinct from the sort that would bring sharp improvements to their bellies and their pocketbooks. The West could only speculate about the big question, namely, whether Gorbachev would resist the separatist movements very much or whether, as a leaked U.S. defence department study argued, he was feigning concern while his master plan unfolded on schedule — a plan to cast aside so many of the ethnic difficulties and other problems by shedding territories until only a core Russian state remained. A friend of mine had been correct when he prophesied, "The danger is that *glasnost* will work all too well and *perestroika* not at all." That is, that the taste for reform, fed by new access to western consumerism, would far outpace the ability of the system to accommodate it, with potentially disastrous results.

Whichever way the events broke, towards unbridled freedom and decentralization, or towards reaction against ethnic nationalism, it was clear that I might well, with luck, be visiting the Soviet Union at perhaps the most exciting time since 1917. The odds were at least rather good that if I got there quickly enough I might be present to see the early stages of some new form of federalism quite different from our own and so complicated as to make the proposed Meech Lake accord seem like "Jingle Bells" by comparison. In the Chinese calendar, 1990 was the Year of the Horse, synonymous with both speed and persistence. I noticed that the Soviets had picked up on the term as well, as in a headline "Will the Year of the Horse solve economic problems?" in *Soviet News & Views*, one of the publications I was now monitoring closely. I shut up my *pied-à-terre* in Kingston and retreated to my permanent home in Toronto to work and worry.

As discussions rolled on, I got to know Andrei Stulov in the Soviet press office in Ottawa, who would be in charge of making the arrangements for my trip. He is a former foreign correspondent for Novosti, the Soviet press agency, and someone I came to appreciate for his subtle command of complex political situations at home and abroad. He reported that there were at least two possible berths for me in Moscow. One was on the weekend supplement of *Izvestia*. The other on the *Literaturnaya Gazeta*, which I was slightly familiar with, mainly because of the cultural mandate explicit in the name; Andrei told me that lately it had broadened its base considerably, becoming especially conspicuous for its investigations of the mafia (a term to which the Soviets impart no ethnic connotation but use to describe all types of organized corruption). I expressed the greatest pleasure at the prospect of either alternative, and the matter went forward with the usual slowness one expects in dealing with any federal bureaucracy, whether situated on the Ottawa River or the Moskva. I continued my daily routine of writing for the *Whig*, using idle moments to study for the trip.

When the official at the Chinese embassy gave me the address of the All-China Journalists' Association in Beijing, he had said that, in his experience, a reply might take anywhere from two weeks to, in exceptional circumstances, perhaps as long as two months. When two months passed and I hadn't heard a peep, I enquired again of my embassy contact, who suggested that I reapply, by telex. I did so and heard nothing for weeks. My departure date was drawing perilously near, I pointed out to the first secretary, who told me to be patient but promised to investigate. I had been in a state of anxiety for some time when one evening, at midnight, I received a telephone call from Beijing. The connection was poor, and the usual several seconds' delay in transmission was complicated by the fact that the man on the other end, though his English was excellent, was having difficulty penetrating my own. The thrust of the conversation was that the association did not have my original application and was surprised therefore to receive my follow-up. My first thought was naturally that my paperwork had been conveniently lost, as by this time the newspapers were full of stories about the crackdown on foreign journalists, as part of the general tightening following the Tiananmen massacre. *The Globe and Mail*'s bureau chief, for example, had written a vivid account of how the secret police had attempted to snatch her off a Beijing street near her home, and the foreign papers were full of dark suggestions about harassment of organizations like the BBC and the

Associated Press. True, those were resident correspondents, who presented a far different menace from a one-time visitor — and a mere literary drone at that. I had no means of gauging the sincerity of the voice at the other end of the wire when he promised to see what he could do. Similarly, the first secretary in Ottawa, when I reported this strange nocturnal chat, seemed to grow less sanguine about my chances. Figuring, I suppose, that subtlety would be lost on me, he said at one point, "You are well to be worried." But he too pledged to keep working on my case.

Nothing happened except that the ticking of the clock grew louder and more emphatic. If I couldn't get into China, then I would have to drastically reduce the scope of my whole mission, for the Soviet part of the trip, though it promised of course to be fascinating in itself, was best seen as part of a single journey that changed complexion as it passed from the European end of the U.S.S.R. (which was becoming more European by the day) to Soviet Asia, through northern China, to Southeast Asia. I enjoy reading other people's travel impressions but had no illusions that anyone would tolerate my own unless they were accompanied by lots of specific information. For events were changing so quickly, I sensed, that whatever I wrote would be obsolete as reportage before I could get it into print, but it might have value as a kind of proto-history, freezing one moment for inspection. I drew up a list of topics — agriculture, the environment, press freedom, birth control and family life, religious tolerance, the climate for artistic expression — about which I would take notes in both the U.S.S.R. and China, hoping to construct a trellis on which to hang comparison. The point was to observe how the two great revolutionary governments of the twentieth century were diverging as the millennium neared, how in the process they influenced, and were influenced by, their neighbours. Without the train trip through the U.S.S.R. and the

People's Republic, there would be nothing to hold my narrative together. As my dealings with bureaucracy grew more labyrinthine, I came to see myself reduced to turning out the political equivalent of one of those *Rolling Stone* stories of the early 1970s, in which the author, by writing an absurdly long account of the near misses, tried to disguise the fact that he had never actually managed to talk to the reclusive rock star he was tracking.

It was now only a couple of weeks before I was due to leave for Moscow. No decision had come down about where I was to work or even where I would be staying, but Andrei reassured me about my visa at least, saying that it would arrive by courier a few days before I was to depart. He also reported optimistically that my requests for various interviews and the like were being worked on in Moscow. For the moment, I felt secure about the Soviet portion of my agenda. The Chinese part was still unsettled. The embassy was now saying that if no progress was made before I left, I could at least begin the whole process anew at the Chinese embassy in Moscow. The very thought sent me into turbo drive, and I threw myself on the mercy of a friendly member of Parliament, who agreed to take up the matter with Joe Clark, the secretary of state for external affairs.

As I found out only later, my request for help came at a piquant moment. The CTV correspondent was the head of the western journalists' group in Beijing, and it seems that he had been talking with External about constraints placed on his members. So a great deal could be read into the apparent foot-dragging about what was after all my modest request simply to travel down the Yangtze. Clark sent a rocket to the North Asia Relations desk at the External building in Sussex Drive and I received the first of many calls from the duty officer there, who seemed to take on my case as a personal project and even got to the point of reading me the cable traffic as his colleague at the Canadian mission in Beijing laid siege to the relevant Chinese official. It took some doing, apparently, but to make a long story short, shorter at least than *Rolling Stone* used to do, after ten days or so I got a message from the Chinese embassy to go to their consulate a few blocks from my house in Toronto and have a journalist's visa stamped in my passport. Hallelujah.

Now it was the turn of the Soviet situation to take an unexpected jump. Word filtered back that neither of the publications previously discussed would be my host after all. The news was still unofficial, but it seemed that I would be seconded to the magazine *Oktyabr*. I had seen it a few times; I can't actually read it, of course, but I knew it to be a small journal (by Soviet standards) of politics and culture, very sombre in its typography and feel but of greater influence than either of those elements would suggest to someone accustomed to western periodicals. About this time there was a minor panic about my visa, which the Soviets claimed had been issued and dispatched but which hadn't arrived (a mix-up on the part of the courier service, as it happened, lasting less than a week in all). Only six days before I was intended to go to Montreal to catch an Aeroflot flight to Moscow, Andrei wired confirming that:

> accommodation, travel arrangements, meetings, and interviews in the U.S.S.R will be provided by *Oktyabr* magazine and the Union of Writers of Russian Federation. As for the moment, almost all of the appointments have been settled according to your previous requests. The preliminary programme will be sent at your attention in a few days.

Still no word where I would be billeted, but he went on to list names and phone numbers for officials of the magazine, one of whom would meet me at the airport.

A few days later, thirty-six hours before my scheduled departure, he wired again, this time with shocking news.

We have just received this date from Moscow an urgent message stating that there are serious management changes which are taking place with *Oktyabr* magazine at this time and they are facing extreme financial difficulties. They have contacted Novosti Press Agency in Moscow stating that unfortunately they are no longer in a position to receive you according to the exchange arrangement with *The Whig-Standard* and have asked Novosti to forward their sincere apologies for having to back out of the deal at this very late date.

He added, "Of course *The Whig-Standard* will no longer be bound by the exchange agreement previously agreed to."

The more likely explanation was obvious, even blatant. The Soviet press had been going through a shake-up. It seemed to extend from *Pravda*, whose old editor, Viktor Afanasyev, had been sacked and replaced by Ivan Frolov, a Gorbachevite, all the way down to the bottom of the pile: a game of realignment important in itself but also vitally symbolic as an indication of changes inside the Kremlin, indeed throughout the society. Wasn't it the case, I put to Andrei at once, that "serious management changes" and "extreme financial difficulties" were in fact just politics?

"Believe me," he said cryptically but in a reassuring tone, "the problem is not you." But that was as far as he cared to go in his explanations or hunches.

Neil Reynolds, who had worked so hard to create the exchange, was aghast, and instantly depressed, when I told him the news. But he's not one to be diverted easily. If the Soviets wouldn't take me in for a month or more as a guest, then the paper would scrape together whatever pennies might remain in forgotten corners of the frozen newsroom budget and send me over as a paying boarder for however long we could afford, so that I could get a feel for the city before the date when my Asia Pacific Foundation money kicked in and I boarded the train to China.

I stayed in Toronto an extra fortnight, with my bags still packed and waiting near the door, while I went through the almost equally aggravating process of dealing with Intours, the Canadian affiliate of Intourist, the Soviet government travel agency. Even on the new pay-as-you-go-in-hard-currency basis, the trip lapsed into doubt more than once, as hotel rooms and domestic train tickets were first possible to obtain, then impossible, then possible again, though barely. I was exhausted and I hadn't even left the house yet. Finally, the day before the office was scheduled to close for the long Easter holiday — my last chance to pull the trip out of the fire — I got the long-awaited telephone call asking me to go to the Intours office in Bloor Street and exercise the privilege of paying over a great deal of money. When I asked where that particular street number was, a voice with deep Slavic intonations informed me that the building was conveniently located "across street from Eve Adult Cinema." So when the latest revised departure date did in fact arrive, I was holding what I prayed would be all the necessary paperwork.

As I was leaving for Montreal I heard the electronic beeping that signals an incoming fax, a sound I had come to dislike, even dread. The message was from the executive director of the Asia Pacific Foundation in Vancouver advising me that there was "no way" I should apply to the Chinese for a journalist's visa. Their intelligence suggested that "the government is getting stricter" as the first anniversary of the events in Tiananmen Square drew near and that "there are several people stranded in Hong Kong."

One thing at a time, I said to myself. This was my new policy.

2
ON THE LOOSE IN MOSCOW

I once departed Canada for France aboard a ship with a Russian crew and came up on deck at dawn the next day to find them doing calisthenics in the rain. That had been my only experience of Soviets in groups. The recollection came back to me at once at Mirabel, that vast empty white elephant of an airport, from which Aeroflot flies to Moscow several times a week. A crowd of a couple hundred people with the distinctive blood-coloured CCCP passports was going home — people with wide Slavic faces, many of them, some of the women with scarves on their heads and a large number of bulky bags or cartons tied with rope, some of the men wearing sweatshirts under their copious blue business suits. At neither end of the departure process — at the check-in counter or at the gate — was it necessary to ask them to form a queue, for they do so automatically day in and day out, though they don't make a religious obligation of neatness the way the British do. Everybody jumps ahead of everybody else while somehow preserving the queue idea, despite the way that the line-up once threatened to become as wide as it was long. There was much weeping and waving goodbye to relatives. One man in his sixties wore not miniature decorations but full-sized tin replicas of his military ribbons but was not otherwise formally dressed (I would see many such people in the U.S.S.R.). Quite aside from questions of age and fashion, the people of that generation look fundamentally different from their sons and daughters and grandchildren. The younger people are simply more European.

The aircraft was bare-bones and the flight long — an all-nighter. Although, in obedience to Gorbachev's drive against alcoholism, a light beer was the only strong drink served, the passengers became restive, shouting across the aisle, socializing, fiddling with all their bloody packages, a number of which, I observed, contained VCRs. If they had held live pigs instead, the level of tranquillity would have been about the same. People were alert with anticipation. When they did settle down to sleep, a few slept with their heads on their crossed arms and their arms on the folding trays in front of them.

Sherenetyevo-2 Aeroport, the one where foreigners usually land, resembles Mirabel in being big and empty and surrounded by farms and patches of boreal woods. In the Soviet Union, many things resemble Mirabel. The wait lasted almost two hours, but when my turn came I breezed through passport control and customs. I struck up a conversation with the clerk while buying currency at the bureau de change, and she told me that the taxi fare to central Moscow should be no more than 15 rubles. Outside I was approached by six drivers in turn, each of whom refused to take me anywhere except for U.S. dollars or Marlboro cigarettes or some combination of the two. Finally I told one of them what they all knew already — that one's foreign currency is scrutinized and counted when one comes in and all hard currency exchanges (but not, it's true, purchases) are recorded on a customs form and must tally on one's departure with the amount remaining. The airport is full of warnings about the danger of selling dollars except at the official kiosks; in the customs hall there were posters with photographs of the black marketeers of the week. It seemed clear that there was great pressure by the government to keep people from using dollars except in those places, run by the government and patronized only by foreigners, where dollars are used exclusively. But no driver would take me on any other basis, and so I lugged my bags back inside and reported my consternation to Intourist. A young woman there shook her head sadly.

"Where do they think they are?" she said. "In Soviet Union or in U.S. of A.?" I responded sympathetically, but kept to myself the realization that I had just stepped into the present and learned my first lesson.

The driver who was shamed or browbeaten into accepting me for rubles was grumpy and sullen as we darted along the Leningradsky Highway, the main road linking the capital and the second city. He swerved in and out of traffic. On both sides were long buildings of various styles and ages, all impressive though many seemed a little shabby, albeit with the shabbiness that comes with long use, not neglect. In the grassy median dividing the highway stood a modern sculpture, dedicated in 1966, that resembles a child's jacks but on a giant scale; it is a memorial to the citizens who defended the city against the Nazis in the Great Patriotic War and is meant to suggest the hedgehogs, or tank traps, which laced the eastern approaches. This stretch of the highway is a showpiece, clearly. We roared past parks and stadiums and the Northern River Terminal, which, with its open arches and high clock tower, suggests what the Ferry Building in San Francisco would have been like if an Italian had designed it. We rumbled past the Petrovsky Palace of Peter the Great, where Napoleon did his hasty logistical planning for the retreat from Moscow. This section was a distant suburb then, and clusters of small single-family homes show that it remained so until the 1920s, perhaps even as late as 1937 when the Moskva was connected to the Volga by canal, and Moscow, after five hundred years as an inland city, finally became a seaport. At the House of the Newlyweds, I spotted a bride getting out of a car with red and blue streamers tied to the rear bumper. The highway had long since dissolved into Leningradsky Prospekt, one of the eleven wide spokes that cross three ring roads before coming together at the Kremlin and Red Square. The driver was still glum when we arrived at the hotel. He wore jeans. Rubles in one pocket, dollars in the other. He made a big display of dredging up change from the one and not the other.

The next morning I watched dawn break over central Moscow from a hotel window on the fifteenth floor. It was like being in a photographer's darkroom, seeing the image come to life in the bath of developer. As the sky grew lighter — but without ever losing the suggestion of pewter — buildings were revealed row after row, following the contours of the river or else standing at attention along either side of the main boulevards. There were large patches of green everywhere, for a surprisingly high percentage of the city's area is given over to parks. Ugly highrises jutted up from the trees in the foreground and in the distance, some with the construction cranes still in place, others dating, I would guess, from the 1960s or early 1970s, when the much reported-on housing crisis was first addressed seriously (but of course never solved).

At a distance, it is not always easy in the U.S.S.R. to distinguish residential buildings from office blocks, owing in part to the absence of signage. One distinctive structure, which I soon learned is one of the seats of the government of the Russian Federation, resembles New City Hall in Toronto except that the two halves of the clamshell are back to back rather than face to face and so take on an X shape when viewed from above. There are also the seven high gothic skyscrapers, serving various functions, built by Stalin, who compared them to the seven hills of Rome. One is the Ukraine Hotel; another is the Ministry of Foreign Affairs and International Trade, which sits across from a little pie-shaped park where I would see a big protest demonstration when Li Peng came to town. A third is the Moskva Hotel, which has mismatched wings. It is said that the architects submitted two plans to Stalin, expecting him to state his preference; when he did not, they built one of each and hoped for the best. As for some of the older structures, I noticed what I later saw confirmed in China as well: how one of the consequences of a revolution is that buildings are put to new uses that never quite eradicate all traces of their original purpose. Moscow's ordinary domestic architecture tends towards long blocks, four or five storeys high and with steep metal-ribbed roofs, such as you expect to see in the workaday parts of Paris and in the centre of the other old European capitals.

This was a special day, the 120th anniversary of Lenin's birth, and I decided to get my sightseeing out of the way and pay my respects to his mummified remains. After a breakfast of coleslaw and what I would call latkes, I bounded out into the crisp morning air for my ritual argument with a cab driver.

"Rubles!" he said. "Rubles I got here. And here and here." He touched all the pockets of his coat and trousers and a zippered bag on the dashboard. We eliminated dollars and cigarettes, leaving him to suggest that I might like to pay in caviar. A coals-to-Newcastle proposition, I would have imagined, though he perhaps meant the white variety often reserved for hard-currency tourists. I decided to walk to the Kremlin.

For a city of 8.5 million, and one so associated with industry, there is little air pollution in Moscow compared with other cities its size. This is no doubt because there are few automobiles, though private ones are becoming more common all the time and cars are one of the most important local manufactures, even if not so important as radio electronics. I walked along the circular roadway and down one of the spokes, the Kalinin Prospekt, a western-style shopping street for which long rows of historic Russian houses were pulled down. Outdoor advertising is still mercifully scarce, though I should think that may not be true much longer if the pace of westernization continues at the present rate, and so I was startled to see an enormous theatre poster plastered on a hoarding along the pavement. Dozens of market stalls, most of them free-enterprise businesses, which the Soviets, in a reversal of nomenclature, call cooperatives, were being set up as I passed along, some with sticky buns and Pepsi (far more common than *Koka-Kola*), others selling manufactured goods from toy soldiers to women's blouses. The merchants did not seem to hustle, the way those in, for instance, an English market would do, but the customers were animated.

The closer I got to the Kremlin, the more soldiers were in evidence, and sailors as well. Officers with briefcases and young conscripts in groups with their girlfriends. It is in the crowds of military personnel, I noticed, that one is most likely to see all the various ethnic groups represented, including the distinctive Mongolians. Flags, too, became increasingly common. I sensed that I had crossed over into official Moscow when I hit a duotone portrait of Lenin, several storeys high, suspended from one of the buildings of the Lenin Library. Just a bit farther on was 50th Anniversary of the October Revolution Square, delineated on one side by a Greek Revival building that once housed indoor equestrian events but is now the Central Exhibition Hall. Then there was a brick gatehouse connected to a bridge over the Alexandrovsky Gardens, which must once have been part of the Kremlin's defensive outerworks. I saw a few civil servants, bureaucrats, and military types flash their security passes to get across. The rest of us were pre-emptively sent down into the sunken garden where, before long, a queue had begun to assume shape. The Lenin Mausoleum wouldn't open for almost two hours yet, but I sensed that this was my opportunity to get in on the ground floor.

I had decided against getting a ticket at the hotel that would have allowed me to jump to the front, for I hoped to find people who spoke English. As luck would have it, the man in front of me possessed English he wished to exercise. He was in his late forties, I would guess, a Moldavian who took frequent trips to Moscow but had never before made the pilgrimage to see the father of the Revolution and the Soviet state. His nine-year-old daughter was with him, dressed in a kind of ski suit, with her long blonde hair tied back with pieces of bobbin lace. She kept staring at me for the exotic foreigner that I am but reverted to excessive shyness when I smiled in response or tried to speak with her. My companion also had a son, now twenty-two, who had recently made him a grandfather. This was an important holiday for the family, though the man went on with genuine sadness about how Moscow was looking so decrepit these days, not full of life and freshly painted as it was when he began coming here fifteen years ago. I couldn't determine to what extent it was his own — our own — advancing years he saw reflected in the surroundings.

The line now stretched for blocks and was suddenly made longer by the arrival of scores of Second World War veterans, some in uniform and others not, some with canes and crutches, most with at least a few medals or decorations, who placed roses on the monument to the unknown soldiers, a place where, on other days, brides and bridegrooms traditionally have their photographs taken. A children's marching band stood to attention, and the old soldiers were then given priority in the slow march around the corner and up the hill towards Red Square and another part of the Kremlin wall. "They no doubt feel bad at being made to go ahead of us", my friend said. But I saw only that they were caught up in their private memories. It is mildly shocking, yet somehow reassuring, to find one's clichés about a country so often revealed as true — never wholly true, mind you, but true nonetheless in their sheer accessibility. First all those peasants at the airport in Montreal, struggling with parcels as lumpy as themselves, and now the fact that the Second World War, in which 20 million Soviets were killed, was still a palpable reality in everyone's life — and I hadn't even got as far as Leningrad, where the fighting had been worse.

As we filed into Red Square the people grew quiet. Hands came out of pockets. One woman quickly combed her hair and straightened her clothes. The clock on the Spasskaya Tower struck 11 a.m. and outside the mausoleum there was a changing-of-the-guard ceremony. The soldiers goose-stepped; I had already seen many soldiers, but these were the first ones whose boots were polished. Two others, on either side of the entrance when we arrived, were armed with old bolt-action rifles with bayonets fixed. Others made last-minute inspections of people's hand bags, looking for cameras, which are forbidden inside, while another soldier moved up and down our part of the line photographing obvious foreigners (he snapped me twice, once, I suppose, because I'm taller than most of the others, and again because I wear a beard). The interior was dark and cool and made of polished granite. We shuffled down some steps, turned a corner, and there he was, illuminated in his glass coffin, wearing a blue silk tie with white dots. He was a small man, and his goatee and the fringe of hair around the sides of his head are sandy red, which surprised me. By no stretch of the language could the corpse be called lifelike, though the fact that it has been preserved as well as this since 1924 does speak kindly of scientific method. Insensitive foreigners are renowned for remarking that the face and hands look like those of a waxwork. On the contrary, it seems to me, the effect suggests wood carving.

One exits the sacred place to walk under a stretch of the Kremlin wall where state heroes, including John Reed, the Harvard alumnus who wrote *Ten Days That Shook the World*, are buried. Revolutionaries, artists, cosmonauts including Yuri Gagarin, have plaques set in the wall and small memorial stones in the turf below. A few foreign names catch the eye, such as that of Big Bill Haywood (1868–1928), the Wobbly from Chicago. Other figures of even higher rank are memorialized by a row of stone busts. Konstantin Chernenko is one of the most recent additions. Stalin is there, too, though he used to rest next to Lenin; Khrushchev had him demoted in 1961.

When I got back to my room I turned on my little shortwave radio to hear Radio Moscow's report of the day's events. Gorbachev was quoted as saying, somewhat pointedly so in the faintness of his praise, "We shall rely on everything lasting in Lenin's intellectual heritage." But the people I was with, young as well as old, seemed to me to be genuinely moved, perhaps even awed, not much ready for revisionism insofar as the cult of Lenin's personality is concerned — a cult that is of course not justified in Lenin's own teachings but not difficult to explain in a culture where icons are such an important form of art. In the ensuing weeks I would meet people who cynically contradicted this first impression of mine.

Later in the day I fell into conversation about what I had seen with a woman who told me that she was first taken to see Lenin by her mother when she was a small girl and so took her own daughter there when the child was about the same age and expects her grandchildren to go one day as well. The notion of such deliberate continuity — as distinct from the unending sameness over which one has no control — seemed quite at odds with the mood of the moment, when everything in the society appeared to be either improving quickly or just as quickly getting worse, but, in any event, changing. Two days later, a forty-nine-year-old Lithuanian stood where I stood and threw two fire-bombs in the direction of Lenin's body. No damage was done. He was arrested.

Events were moving so rapidly, in fact, that our memory of the present chronology is understandably jumbled. So perhaps I should pause here to give a more exact context to these remarks and observations.

At the time of which I write, Gorbachev was settling into the new presidential powers he had given himself and recently had gone so far in the direction of western politics as to create the post of presidential press secretary. Politically and economically, chaos was barely being restrained. Ethnic tensions in Azerbaijan may have cooled, but the Lithuanians had declared themselves independent, forcing Gorbachev to cut off most shipments of natural gas and virtually all their supply of oil. His legal grounds for doing so were unclear, as there was simply no legislation on the matter one way or the other, but the action was better than sending tanks; everyone was on tenterhooks waiting to see whether he could force the Lithuanians into a referendum on the succession question followed by a slow transition over five years. The Lithuanians had just responded with an embargo of their own involving those products, such as small electric motors and television tubes, on which their factories had been given a near monopoly long ago.

Back in Moscow, Gorbachev's adversaries were snapping at him, not only the communist old guard who distrust reform, a group we heard less about in the West, but also the more highly profiled radicals who felt that the reforms were not proceeding nearly so quickly as they might. The most conspicuous of these was of course Boris Yeltsin, the brusque one-time construction foreman and former mayor of Moscow who periodically would accuse Gorbachev of becoming a dictator and who clearly wanted to set himself up as president of the core state, the Russian Federation that accounts for half of the U.S.S.R.'s population and four-fifths of its territory. At this time, a few months before he succeeded in that goal, his image in the West was still coloured by the visit he had paid to the U.S. and elsewhere in 1989, when he drank and talked prodigiously, and coloured, too, by an incident in Moscow shortly afterward when he claimed he was abducted by thugs and thrown in the river. In Britain, therefore, he was being seen by some in much the same light as George Brown was regarded in the 1960s, while in Canada his big square head and rough-hewn manners often recalled Eugene Whelan, Pierre Trudeau's perpetual agriculture minister. In fact, a closer approximation would have been a cross between William Lyon Mackenzie and René Lévesque.

When I arrived, Moscow was abuzz with the imminent swearing-in of a new mayor, Gavrill Popov, a free-market economist who had vowed to lease properties and businesses to organizations and individuals and otherwise move decisively towards a more workable economy, knowing that what Moscow does must inevitably be done in other cities and regions. When I got to know several leading journalists at Novosti, I asked whether these leases would be for long terms and whether they might one day be converted to freehold private property. "At the start, just leases", I was told. "But wait a few months." This was an answer I was to hear to several questions. For example, at that time there was still, officially, only one political party. But at the urging of Yegor Ligachev, the leading conservative in the Politburo, a number of radicals had been expelled before they could resign, and they were poised to set up their own party. They were already arguing about what the name on the letterhead should be. Similarly, a green party was positioned to begin fielding candidates in the autumn, and there was a royalist party aborning, hoping to restore order by restoring the monarchy, as had happened in Spain. "In two months, you'll see, there will be a dozen parties." The number, like the timeframe, was arbitrary, but the thrust was accurate enough. There would no doubt be parties galore — reform and counter-reform, radical and reactionary, ones on specific issues, perhaps even religious ones; in time, they would probably be rationalized along economic and ethnic lines.

Most everyone I talked to was weary of the present and impatient for change, almost any kind of change, and yet at the same time fearful of what the immediate future would be like. Americans tend to interpret this unrest as a frantic desire to embrace Americanism, but that of course is ridiculous. People pursue some measure of democracy not out of the Americans' cloying sentimentality about voting for its own sake but as a means of seeing a mixed economy in which their subsidized housing, unlimited education, and free social programmes might be enhanced by a convertible currency and a little decent food. The currency question is exceptionally thorny. To make the ruble convertible into dollars, Deutschmarks, sterling and so forth would be instantly to erode the people's pensions and savings. (And because there is so little they can buy in the shops, Soviets are champion savers, having put away 340 billion rubles in the state bank even though the interest is only 1.5 per cent —this in addition to an estimated 200 billion rubles in "under the bed" savings.) Yet inflation is quickly eating up this pile anyway. In 1989 the government deficit was estimated by an outside specialist at 120 billion rubles, up from only 20 billion in 1982; to service the debt, Moscow simply prints more currency at the rate of 50 million rubles a day, 18 billion rubles a year. The most imaginative idea voiced to date has been to back the ruble with gold, of which the U.S.S.R. is the second-largest producer, thus bringing all the world's savings and investment rushing in. Absurd of course, but wonderful. But the reason Gorbachev, the liberal reformer, can exist, and by existing save us by winding down the Cold War, is that he is a moderate who needs immoderates such as Yeltsin or the gold-bugs to play himself off against. The phrase "five years" comes to his lips as easily, and as frequently, as "two months" came to the lips of my newfound acquaintances in the press. I can only guess whether this carries an echo, in listeners' ears, of all those long-ago five-year plans.

Embarrassed by the collapse of the exchange with *Oktyabr*, Andrei Stulov in Ottawa had put me in touch with two of his friends at Novosti, who promised to help arrange some interviews and meetings, including one at *Oktyabr* itself, where I hoped I could play upon their minor guilt, transforming it into access to some of the writers and painters I desired to meet. I had also asked to observe the meeting between Gorbachev and Li Peng when the Chinese leader arrived in Moscow to pay his respects and discuss border problems, but the indications were that this would be difficult to arrange. Back when the faxes were flying furiously between Moscow and Ottawa and Ottawa and me, the response had been favourable when I sought permission to interview Yeltsin and a few other politicos, such as the minister of culture, Vasily Zakharov.

But in the present situation the possibilities had receded. Before I could get in to see him, for example, Zakharov had been replaced by Nikolai Gobenko, putting me back at zero, though there was a much bigger factor working against me. "They're trying to keep foreign journalists away from politicians if they can", said Slava Bogdanov of Novosti's North American department with an admirable and characteristic frankness. He had preceded Stulov at the press attaché's job in Ottawa but had returned home in 1988. He speaks perfectly idiomatic English and is the resident expert on English Canada. When I met him he had just returned from three weeks in Vancouver and was soon to lead a delegation to a symposium in Ottawa.

Novosti is a difficult news organization to categorize. It is large, employing several thousand journalists to TASS's several hundred, and in further distinction to TASS, which provides the official news from the party and the government, it is "public", which the West usually interprets as meaning merely "semi-official". It publishes informal books and slick pamphlets about every aspect of the U.S.S.R. in a variety of languages and responds to requests for customized stories from the overseas media, including even *The Whig-Standard*, which sometimes prints Novosti material on its Forum page. More important, it runs its own network of correspondents both domestically and worldwide, and acts as a clearing house, though not as a telegraphic news agency like TASS or Canadian Press. It is also the publisher of the important *Moscow News*, which is considered not just radical but sometimes quite fearless. Recently it has ventured into television as well. For example, it buys a regular ninety minutes of airtime from the state network for the broadcast of such programmes as the first-ever look inside KGB headquarters in Dzerzinsky Square. Its highly distinctive building in Zoubovski Boulevard, opening on a courtyard and with terraced balconies, is also a communications centre from which Soviet figures and foreign heads of state address press conferences. "During the Moscow Olympics," Bogdanov explained, sitting in a large meeting room with a bar, "this was full of TV monitors, and many distinguished sports journalists followed the various competitions from here, never venturing outside." He pantomimed the chugging of alcoholic beverages and laughed wryly.

His colleague, Alexey Lipovetsky, is also part of the North American desk, which with thirty personnel is quite the smallest of Novosti's branches. He is forty-one, somewhat rumpled, with a drooping black moustache and a sly, cynical wit. Trained at the Moscow Institute for Foreign Languages to be a simultaneous translator, he is the agency's specialist on Quebec and speaks English with a Québécois accent. He is the most experienced and productive kind of journalist, the sort you find a few of in the top ranks of the profession in every country: unstoppably curious, at ease with all types of people, and with a love of imparting all the accurate information he has at his fingertips but with a discriminating filter that automatically weeds out the patently false or illogical. We spent a good bit of time together, talking about, among other things, the press. More than a need for shop talk motivated my enquiries. It was clear that the press had become an engine of change as well as an instrument to measure it. One day we were walking thought Gorky Park, very near where Alexey grew up. It was spring but it seemed like an early autumn day; there were few people about, and the Ferris wheel and other amusements were silent.

"The press is at the leading edge of the idea of the free market", he said. "Consider the case of *Pravda*." The official party newspaper is by no means the juggernaut it formerly was (and perhaps remains in the heads of most westerners who have occasion to consider the subject at all). Officials, and journalists who follow developments in the

Central Committee, still consume it and try to decipher its levels of suggestion and implication, but millions of ordinary readers have dropped away. "As soon as a person realizes that there is something better, he changes his habits", Alexey said. Any publication that professes to throw light into the dark corners of societal administration, or even chronicle the fresh evidence of change all around, is the beneficiary. The most remarkable success story, though remarkable is scarcely an adequate word, is an eight-page tabloid weekly whose name, translatable as *Arguments and Facts*, is a fair description of its method as well as its content. Four years after it was founded, its circulation stood at 34 million, the largest of any periodical in the world. In addition, there are the underground papers, so called even though they have ceased to be *samizdat* ventures, produced clandestinely and distributed furtively, hand to hand.

"I was curious about how many there are, and so one day recently I asked the librarian at our agency how many of these we subscribe to", Alexey said. "It seems that we buy 210 of them. By no means all of these are from Moscow, of course, but no doubt there are many others we do not receive." One of the better-known examples recently riveted attention on itself by publishing an irreverent investigation of Mrs Raisa Gorbachev's personal spending habits. (As I write this sentence, I look out the window and see an articulated lorry carrying rolls of newsprint and am reminded that this is another of the commodities included in the embargo against the Lithuanians.)

Some publications not previously considered radical have begun to take on a patina of radicalism. *Nedelya*, the weekly supplement of the decidedly middle-of-the-road *Izvestia*, is the obvious example. Only a thoroughgoing cynic, however, would suggest that they have done so solely in an attempt to lure readers by catering to fashion. Yet there is no doubt at least as to which are the true radical journals.

They are the weekly newspaper *Moscow News* and the weekly magazine *Ogonyok*. I was counting on the freemasonry of journalists to gain me admittance to both places.

The *News* was founded in 1930 and is owned jointly by Novosti and an organization called the Union of Soviet Societies for Friendship and Cultural Relations with Foreign Countries. Accordingly there are editions in English, French, German, Spanish, Hungarian, Estonian, and Arabic, with an aggregate circulation fo 300,000, as compared with 500,000 copies of the Russian-language original. The offices are situated on one of the most advantageous pieces of real estate in Moscow. On a bright moderate day, too warm for a coat, too cool for just a pullover, I decided to walk there, a distance of several kilometres, rather than add to my knowledge of Moscow's extraordinarily ornate metro stations.

Gorki Street begins within easy sight of the Kremlin and runs northwest. Near the foot is the National Hotel, built at the turn of the century and once the U.S. embassy, before the Revolution forced the move to their present building in Tchaikovsky Street (and of course before the attempted new one, which they discovered was riddled with hidden listening devices and so must raze even before they've finished constructing it). Farther up is the headquarters of TASS, the telegraph agency and news service; its corner building is recognizable instantly by the huge globe over the entrance; the globe is supposed to revolve, but it stopped working twenty some years ago and has never been repaired. But mostly this wide and orderly boulevard, with some architecture going back to Napoleonic times, is lined with the city's, and the country's, finest shops; mews and side streets contain hidden parks and luxury flats. Many buildings are marked with commemorative tablets, each with a portrait relief, showing some historical figure who once lived there, and it seems clear that there will be cause for more such plaques in future generations, for this is the haunt of the famous and the well rewarded. One richly decorated white building, I was told, is full mainly of ballet stars. My informant told me the flats have particularly high ceilings; I replied that this is probably best in the circumstances.

More than any other district, Gorki Street shows the extraordinary old European city that underlies our preconceived notions about Moscow, showing it to be the poor sister of London or Paris but a full sibling when it comes to complexity, age, size, style, and even grandeur. Which makes it all the more significant that the *Moscow News* should occupy one corner of Gorki Street and Pushkin Square, the most westernized place in this westernized boulevard. Across the way, for example, is the world's largest and by no means most unpleasant McDonald's, owned by George Cohon of Toronto and employing 600 Muscovites. On opening day recently they faced a crowd of 30,000 customers and, as one of my new acquaintances put it, "ascended quickly to the record book of Guinness." Whenever I passed by during my stay hundreds of people were queuing to get in — queuing eagerly, it seemed to me, without the resignation that always appears to mark the faces of those passing their time in the constant lineups for staple goods. But kittycorner, outside the *News*, there is sometimes a large crowd hungry for something more nourishing. When the paper first comes out each Tuesday, its sixteen pages are pinned up in display cases running along the side of the building, and citizens jostle one another for the chance to read the news. That side of Pushkin Square is a traditional spot for such anticipation, and a perplexing variety of newspapers is vended there.

Many Soviet papers organize their physical plants on the German plan, with one composing room and one stand of presses working round the clock on a co-operative basis to produce newspapers of different sorts and allegiances, each of which maintains only its editorial shop as a separate operation apart from the rest. The *Moscow News* is different, though. It has its own exclusive plant, which is located some distance from the editorial rooms in Pushkin Square. The arrangement is made all the more awkward because the *News*, like virtually all the Soviet press, has not yet progressed to computerized production.

Two months before my visit, the offices were gutted by a fire, and I found the staff holed up in temporary quarters in an adjoining building whose lobby still smelled strongly of smoke. "There was no suggestion of arson", explained Sergei Volovets, one of the editors and the paper's former London correspondent, when I located him at the end of a slot-like room, perhaps two metres wide and six metres deep. "It was an accident. But the fire was several storeys up, and the fire brigade poured so much water on the blaze that the floors below were ruined too." Hundreds of readers from many countries contributed to a relief fund. "We hope to get permission from city council to start rebuilding soon", he said. "The climate here makes it difficult to begin work of this sort except in the summer, and we must be finished before the cold comes, because the building we are in now has no heat." City hall has bandied about the phrase "two months".

The *News* is the sort of newspaper that you want to hug or applaud. It was quick to attack the Chinese for the outrage at Tiananmen Square and was critical of Li Peng during his visit. It has been hard on both Gorbachev and Ligachev on point after point, sometimes even recklessly so, to judge by the English-language edition I read, but there is a consistent logical voice behind the formidable amount of information it provides, information, it would seem, that is often available nowhere else. One of its memorable scoops dealt with two former prosecutors who became members of the Supreme Soviet only to discover organized corruption in the highest echelons of that chamber; the pair narrowly avoided being charged by the attorney general after the *News* began printing their revelations. Similarly, it was the *News* that finally proved that the wartime massacre of Polish officers at Katyn, an event the Soviet Union had always attributed to the Nazis, was in fact the work of Stalin's henchmen, just as the Poles had suspected for fifty years. "And our stand on Lithuania differs from the official line in a number of respects", Volovets said with a smile of understatement. The paper is too extreme for the Cubans and at one point was banned even in Hungary.

What struck me most in the issues I read was a certain trenchancy, even down to the back page devoted to culture, where I one day found this item by a contributor named Alexander Vershinin:

> It is a cultural event when new books appear on a library shelf. When books disappear from the shelves — this too can be an important cultural event. But the main thing is to know what will be put there instead.
>
> I got a call from the library where I used to lecture about the theatre: "Tomorrow Brezhnev's works will go into the shredder. If you want them, you'd better hurry."
>
> I went and stared at the shelves. Hundreds of heavy volumes — the majority being red. The paper was high-grade, the covers were excellent, and the minimum printed copy runs were 100,000. But what was most remarkable were the titles. For about an hour I rummaged through them, getting pretty dusty in the process.
>
> Brezhnev, *On Internationalism and Friendship of Peoples* — 150,000 copies. Brezhnev, *The Virgin Lands* — 3,250,000 copies. Brezhnev, *Rebirth* —

3,250,000 copies. Brezhnev, *Following Lenin's Course* in nine volumes — each 300,000 copies. Brezhnev, *Matters of Topical Interest in the CPSU Ideological Work*, in two volumes, 1978 — 100,000. Brezhnev, *Matters of Topical Interest in the CPSU Ideological Work*, 1979, in two volumes, second edition, enlarged, 1979 (the only change is the Fourth Star of the Hero in the portrait) — 300,000.

On Lenin and Leninism — 100,000 copies. *Guarding Peace and Socialism* — 100,000. *It is for the Young to Build Communism. The Party and the Government's Concern about the People's Well-being*, book two. *The Party and the Government's Concern about the People's Well-being*, book three, part two. Ponomaryov, *Selected Works*. Romanov, *Selected Works*. Ustinov, *Selected Works*. Andropov, *Selected Works*. Grishin, *Selected Works*. Kunayev, *Selected Works*. Shcherbitsky, *To Master the Leninist Style of Work*. Chernenko, *The People and the Party are United*.

For the people, about the people, with the people, but, alas, the ungrateful ignoramuses didn't appreciate it. The books are six, 10, 15, 20 years old and none of them have ever been opened. The jackets are brand new. The cards are clean with no names of any readers in them. And this, although ours is the country with the biggest number of readers.

I collected books weighing more than 100 kilograms. Not to change for Dumas, no. I shall put them in the house, admire them, give them to friends as presents on May 1, November 7. I wanted to take a taxi, but it was impossible. I caught an off-duty truck. We threw all this into it and hauled it to my apartment. Kids were playing in the yard — they rushed to help me. They dragged and panted: "Oh, uncle, where did you buy so much?" No, kids, I didn't purchase this. This is a present to the people. This is priceless. These turn thousands of square kilometres of fine forests into useless paper. This is our damned past. This is us.

I couldn't find Rashidov. Apparently, he came along a bit late. So much garbage! The paper is white, the covers are red and my hands are black. Only with great difficulty did I manage to get them clean.

"One of our biggest problems", Sergei Volovets told me, "is that we can't get enough paper to print on. There is a crisis of newsprint. To fill our needs we would have to buy paper from Finland for hard currency and — ". He made a gesture to show the difficulty of that alternative. The U.S.S.R. has no newspaper recycling plants, but the Austrians and Finns sell to third parties the newsprint that they have recycled from Soviet sources. Space for news in the paper has been further restricted by Soviet journalism's discovery of advertising — mostly for foreign airlines, to judge by the *Moscow News*. "But our advertising revenues will be only $150,000 this year, and the biggest part of that goes back to the government in taxes."

Two western journalists, one American and the other British, had recently published a long article in *The New York Review of Books* entitled "How Free is the Soviet Press?" based on a couple of weeks' travel and talking to people. Quite high up in the piece they identified Yegor Yakovlev, the editor-in-chief of the *Moscow News*, as "an associate of Gorbachev". It is precisely because of its opposition to Gorbachev, for supposedly being insufficiently committed to speedy reform, that the *News* is so popular and so important.

To find out about the pace and the twists in Gorbachev's plans, one is more likely to turn not to *Pravda* or *Izvestia* but to a magazine called *Ogonyok*, whose masthead used to proclaim that it was the journal of the Central Committee, a statement that has been dropped. *Ogonyok* is edited by Vitali Korotich, who kept making and then cancelling appointments with me as he tried to determine just what the status of my visit was. The day of the last scheduled meeting, word came down that he had been called away to the Central Committee on urgent business; I made a mental note of the phrase so that I can use it myself on those occasions when "a slight indisposition" is simply not a good enough excuse.

Korotich is a well-known poet and nonfiction writer from the Ukraine, but most assuredly not part of the stereotypical Ukrainian right wing. His literary life has permitted him a lot of travel to the West, including several trips to Canada, and he once spent six months at the UN, resulting in a book about the U.S. whose title could be translated as *The Ugly Face*; he has also written about France and about the life of Siberian oilfield workers. Early on he saw in the still-young Gorbachev a latent streak of liberalism, and formed an alliance. It is said, no doubt with a little exaggeration, that they speak on the telephone daily.

When Korotich got involved in it, *Ogonyok* was a small general interest and cultural monthly with a circulation of 50,000 or 75,000. It now has 3.3 million readers who have been lured to it by its endless exposés about bureaucrats and the "mafia" and also by its hints about Gorbachev's current thinking and the delicate state of *perestroika*. It was in *Ogonyok*, for example, that the first sign of the anti-radical backlash in the army appeared.

So how free *is* the Soviet press? The communist party and the government still appoint the top editors, still impose circulation ceilings, and still install censors who sit in editorial offices — though admittedly the censors have little to do these days, in the present mood of freedom. As I write this the controversial Press Bill, the first in Soviet history, is meandering its way towards law in a few months' time. Its main provision is to permit individuals or collections of individuals to found and publish newspapers or periodicals of their own, without sanction by, or hindrance from, the party or the state.

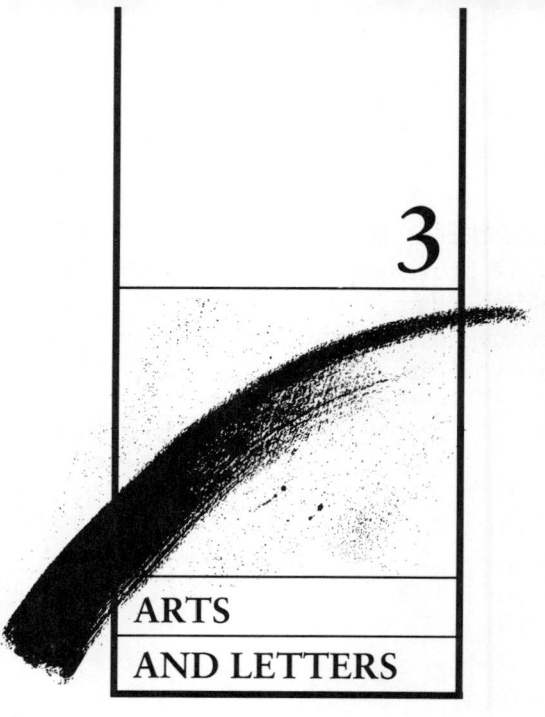

3
ARTS AND LETTERS

If the press is in a state of flux, changing and growing according to no discernable plan beyond whatever tomorrow might bring, so too are the arts — but for some additional reasons. When liberalism is in the ascendant, art and culture always tend to flourish, as the energy pent up in more restrictive times is given an appreciative outlet, with results that are variously youthful, contagious, and self-intoxicating. The sexual revolution that is sputtering to a regressive and ignoble conclusion in the West, as AIDS and other factors bring an end to a long holiday of public sensuality, is just beginning in the U.S.S.R. Sex and nudity are now almost de rigueur in Soviet feature films and especially on the stage, "even in pieces from Chekhov and scenes from Shakespeare", I was told. But this also has to do with the depoliticization of art and the concurrent rise of the free market in culture and everything else. Public art, sanctioned art, subsidized art — it must still be justified by what I more than once heard called *conjuncture*, or theoretical grounding in the social here-and-now for reasons of national pride. But partly this is force of habit. Soviet readers, for example, *like* novels about politics, old ones and new ones, indigenous or foreign. Yet the demands that art be used to laud and justify the achievements of socialism — the basis for social realism in art — is way in the past, and much of the job of simply promoting politics and community has been taken over by the newly free press. The bureaucracy is therefore cutting back on some kinds of arts spending. Gorbachev took a bold pro-arts initiative, for example, when he appointed a prominent stage and cinema actor as culture minister. One of the minister's first important interviews revealed that many theatre companies would have to find free-market ways of contributing to their own keep. He also noted, with what mixture of emotions I found it impossible to know, that the trend of so many professional artists letting themselves be subsumed into politics and public service was, well, a sort of double-edged sword. (Not long after my trip, the new culture minister led a performing artists' protest against the state of Soviet culture — in effect, against his own policies.)

So I set out to try to learn something of the current state of the arts, not just their political economy but also, so to say, their texture. I began at the point of easiest access, the offices of *Oktyabr*. They are located in Pravda Street, so named because much of the opposite side of the quaint tree-lined boulevard is occupied by that newspaper, and its giant printing plant and various affiliated buildings, like the "palace of culture" (concert hall and all-purpose performing arts centre) and "sanitarium" (health club) for the use of its employees, such as most of the largest industries, unions, and professions enjoy —

another manifestation of the older, more rigidly planned approach to culture.

Oktyabr is in an old mansion with a large shady garden in front. Inside it looks like literary magazines everywhere: second-hand furniture; proofs, files, and manuscripts in permanent disarray; a few dedicated people, though more than one would find on a similar journal in the West. I drank glasses of tea with Nina Loshkareva, the deputy editor-in-chief, and Inessa Nazarova, the executive secretary. Another employee, a young copy-editor, married to an editor at an encyclopaedia publisher, kindly volunteered to take me the following day on a tour of Old Moscow, which carries many of the same associations as Bloomsbury, with a little bit of Soho thrown in. It was once the student quarter, but Moscow University long ago relocated to the Lenin Hills outside the city.

In this part of Moscow, abutting the famous Arbat, with its colourful shops, small cafés, and ensnared tourists, there are unexpected pieces of the architectural past, including a great many with literary, artistic or musical associations, around every corner. One stately classical mansion in Vorovsky Street is said to be the model for the home of the Rostov family in *War and Peace*; it is used as a kind of retreat by the Association of Soviet Writers. Near by is the House of Writers, a club and meeting hall, where I was invited a number of times. It was formerly a Masonic lodge, and the rich panelling in the dining room is carved with such motifs as the double-headed eagle of the czars, while the cellar is a bar. I sensed that this is to Soviet writers what the Groucho Club is to English ones — there is a delicate ego-system at work there.

The area is rich in museums dedicated to such figures as Pushkin. When one of the foreign embassies, which are also centred here, wanted to build on a small park, the protesters erected a sign indicating that the tree in the centre of it had strong associations with Pushkin, thereby mocking themselves while preserving the spot. We also stopped at the place where Pushkin was married. My guide called it the Church-of-Jesus-Christ-Going-Up-in-the-Air, which I took to be the Church of the Ascension. It is being restored, but there was some debate as to whether it should be a museum or a living church; there was recent precedent for either, as Gorbachev has returned some old monasteries to the Russian Orthodox Church and caused some of them to be restored as well. Which brings home the fact that there are political currents even in the museum field. Only in the past few months had the state made a museum of the house occupied from 1843 to 1846 by Alexander Gertsen, the revolutionary editor who spent most of his exile in England. He has risen from relative obscurity partly because it turns out that he was the first person to employ the word *glasnost* in the contemporary sense.

However refreshing such communion with the past — and to me it is one of the major pleasures of Moscow, to an extent that quite took me by surprise — my task was to report on the present. And so, over the course of several more days, I set out to make my rounds.

Book publishing was another point of entry. Western writers and readers all know the stories of how the classic Russian writers are revered, and even read, by the true proletariat as well as by the allegorical working class, and how contemporary Soviet writers, or those who carry the seal of approval, see their works gobbled up in editions of many hundreds of thousands of copies; how writers are debated, argued about, and accorded signs of importance such as in North America are only ever given to figures in big business, entertainment, sport, and crime. There is some truth in this supposition, but of course the situation is rather more complicated — as bad as it is good. In any event, the kind of Soviet publishing North Americans are most familiar with, the English-language editions of Soviet and western writers associated with Progress Books in Toronto or International Publishers in New York — the loving editions of Whitman, Steinbeck, Langston Hughes, and so on, with their thin flimsy paper, mundane design, and quaint 1950s hot-lead typography — turns out to be another area — surprise — that is undergoing rapid change. Such was what I learned from a visit to Alexei Faingar, one of the editorial department chiefs at Progress Publishers, the state's foreign-literature works and, with 1,500 employees, the country's biggest publishing house. This year it will bring out 600 titles in fifty languages, and another hundred in Russian, in the fields of literature, history, politics, law, and the sciences.

Faingar is a beautifully tailored man in his fifties, polylingual, relaxed, and sophisticated, with the look of a shrewd negotiator and a keen judge of a fluid marketplace. He looks like any European publisher you would expect to find at the Frankfurt Book Fair. We met in the boardroom.

"How are the books selected? Ah, that is a complicated process, but I would say that we rely one-half on our editors here and one-half on outside specialists living in Moscow. The latter may work in some academical institution, as in, to take an example, the Institute for the United States and Canada. As for ourselves here, I offer as an illustration my own department, which is that concerned with essays, works of quality journalism, and so on. We try to use every possible source of such literature, even private sources. We read foreign periodicals, especially the book-review sections; we have a special department for ordering what might be of interest, and we have [hard] currency for the purpose. As a result, we can plan a year's activities." When he spoke, in early spring 1990, he was engaged in planning his 1992 releases. On subsequent days I spent some time in the foreign-language bookshop in the same building. Recent releases in English literature included a selected writings of Evelyn Waugh, a lesser novel of Robert Penn Warren's, and an anthology of journalism with the status of literature that included a long extract from Defoe's *Journey thro' the whole of Great Britain*. I perceived no common thread with respect to ideology — perhaps those days are gone — nor with respect to the usefulness of the texts as teaching aids. Taste was the only basis for selection obvious to me.

The typical press run for a work of mass literature is 50,000 copies, a figure that corresponds roughly to Canadian numbers if you allow for the fact that Canada has less than 10 per cent of the U.S.S.R.'s population. For the blockbusters, as many as half a million copies might be printed, while for specialized or scientific works, the total might be as few as 5,000 copies. Soviet publishers don't ordinarily maintain extensive backlists of popular titles, but print a book hoping to sell it out so they can move on to the next. People shop for books as they shop for food, gobbling up whatever's available on that particular day. So at least some small part of what outsiders take to be the average Soviet's voracious appetite for culture and learning is the buy-now-and-hoard-for-tomorrow-it-will-be-gone mentality. (I keep remembering the sight of a stylishly attired woman on a trolley-bus, opening her expensive western handbag in search of a five-kopeck ticket to reveal a half dozen of some vegetable — it looked like a cousin of the rutabaga — caked in mud, just as they had come from the farmer's field. Whenever Soviets see valuable goods being vended, they join the queue and buy some, for these goods will soon be worth more than rubles.)

Not all that long ago it was commonly supposed in the West that Soviet publishers of foreign writers were motivated by a desire to show the West in an unfavourable light and would undertake athletic feats of editing to satisfy this ulterior motive. I remember Peter C. Newman showing me the Russian-language edition of *The Canadian Establishment*; it was a mere fraction of the length of the original, presumably because it retained only the material about Bay Street operators calculated to suggest that they are the norm of Canadian society. More recently, I know, the Soviets have published, without any interference or manipulation, Canadian writers whose unflattering views of the Soviet Union are well known. One house, for example, has made a selected poems of Al Purdy available. Which is not to suggest that the Soviets have rushed to find a special affinity with Canada, whatever geo-cultural logic there might be in such twinning. "Our geography section has published such writers as Farley Mowat on your northern regions," said Faingar on cue, "and I read and enjoyed his book on the Second World War [*And No Birds Sang*], but in the end we didn't publish it. I confess that Canadian literature is our weak point. We learn not enough of it." He left the impression that Canadians themselves must take more of the initiative. This led us to discuss the whole question of payments received by authors, a topic in which I have a permanent interest, though one, sadly, that is rather more theoretical than not.

In the past, Soviet publishers would withhold royalties on Russian translations of western books but permit an author to come in person and collect some or all of the money in his or her account, for spending inside the U.S.S.R. In the 1960s many a fur hat and many a case of vodka were bought under pressure of deadline by poor drudges from the West with rubles burning a hole in their pockets. The clerks at the GUM Department Store in Red Square must have seen them coming for miles. But in May 1973, a dozen years before *glasnost*, the Soviets finally joined the Geneva Copyright Convention and now dutifully send foreign authors their royalties on books published after that date.

Payments are made in the foreign currency of the writer's preference. Some time soon — a few months or a few years? I wasn't able to pin anyone down — they are expected to become signatories of the Berne Convention as well and will then pay up on books predating 1973. Of course, publisher-author relations have always been touchy, with some writers, Americans particularly, refusing to co-operate with the U.S.S.R. Tom Wolfe, for example, would not permit Progress to print a large portion of *The Right Stuff*, though he has relented and is allowing them to produce his novel *The Bonfire of the Vanities*.

In the West, writers receive a percentage — usually 10 per cent — of the retail price of the book, but in the U.S.S.R. they are paid according to the number of "signatures", which in the Soviet equation amounts to approximately twenty-five pages of typescript, as well as the "circulation", or size of the print run; actual sales, or the speed of sales, is irrelevant. This allows the publisher to calculate the sum in advance (and pay 25 per cent of it on signing the contract, 35 per cent when typesetting is completed, and the final 40 per cent on publication). But all this may change soon, for the whole process of getting the books to the readers is undergoing dramatic alteration, like so much else in the country. Formerly, all newly printed books from all publishers went to the Book Union, a monopoly trade organization that supplied all the shops and took one-quarter of the retail price. And those prices, like all other financial details, were set out by Goskompechat, the state committee for publishing, printing, and bookselling. "But two days ago", Faingar informed me, "the directors of three hundred houses met in this building to establish the Soviet Publishing Association", with the purpose of finding a way to arrive at prices based on what the market will bear. "This may be the beginning of the end of the Book Union's monopoly on bookselling", he said. "Maybe in a year's time there won't even be a state committee for publishing." Others I talked to were less hopeful.

Far more so, I believe, than in literature, Moscow at this time is particularly rich in the visual arts, and I was fortunate to be able to see a variety of new work and various related activity. I was most pleased, for example, by a visit to an art auction preview, though it was a rather anaemic affair by western standards, held in an ugly, mostly vacant light-industrial space down by the river that bore the same relationship to the London and New York sale rooms as the dreariest Moscow café bears to a four-star restaurant. But it was rewarding in a number of ways. Although without doubt much of Russia's moveable past — books, pictures, antiques, and the like — was destroyed during successive revolutions and wars, it was probably not subjected to a deliberate policy of mass destruction except briefly when the Bolsheviks took power (quite a different situation from China's during the days of the Red Guards). Rather, it simply became irrelevant; Lenin's mission after all was to build a new world; *new* was the operative word. That the export of all art and antiquities of the remotest consequence was prohibited for so many decades contributed to the strength of the pool, as did the low level of disposable income. Now, in the second-hand bookshops, and not just those found among the upscale souvenir places in the Arbat, the European custom of selling old books under the same roof as pictures and prints would seem to be creating some bargains for collectors. Nothing of great importance in the art-historical sense, perhaps, but plenty of attic clutter from late czarist times, which in shop windows or in the auction preview I mentioned hangs side by side with minor contemporary work — not amateur but not really professional either — from which it is often indistinguishable in terms of manner.

This is an important point, it seems to me: the sheer force of accumulated tradition is a question young artists there must come to terms with. The response that painters and sculptors formulate is one of the many factors that determine whether they will be official artists or avant-garde ones. The former term has not changed its meaning much under *perestroika*; such artists are not like those in the Stalin era, working on huge murals of heroic workers marching behind tractors, but they do resemble the social realists of old in that they are members of the U.S.S.R. Artists' Guild or a similar body. *Avant-garde* takes a little more defining, and I was lucky in having a skilled explainer who could also get me inside studios representative of the two types of artist.

Maria Pustukhova, who is twenty-six, was born in the closed city of Vladivostok in the Far East when her mother was the first woman in local television there; her father was a creative writer who then became a journalist with *Pravda*, which brought the family to Moscow when Maria was twelve. Shopping trips to Prague have helped her to cultivate the western appearance of Soviet young people, at least of those in the big cities, but her look is altogether more stylish than the usual blue jeans and Reeboks. She is an art critic and art historian. "I live for the avant-garde", she told me as a plain statement of fact, without any of the faux-drama such phrases carry in English. She and I scampered along to a small street behind Starokonyushenny Lane, where the Canadian embassy is located, to the two-room basement apartment that Alexei Mironov uses as his sculpture studio. The space, quite separate from the flat where he lives, in another part of the city, is crammed with works in stone, clay, wood, plaster, and various metals. Sometimes a painter friend uses the space as well, and as we descended the dark steps we caught the faint smell of turps, which all studio-hounds love, whether they admit it or not.

Mironov, who is not yet thirty, got a sound start. Both his parents were recognized artists, and he graduated from the Stroganov College of Industrial Design when he was twenty-two. For monumental works he sometimes employs assistants, in the traditional manner. Maria told me going in, "He is very rich for an artist" — to the extent that he owns an automobile, or did until quite recently. By Soviet standards he is even richer in experience: he has been to the West. He is represented in several public collections in the U.S.S.R. and in private ones there and elsewhere. In the past couple of years he has been able to accept invitations to visit Britain — first Glasgow, then London — where he had pieces in group exhibitions.

I noticed that like many of the young artists whose work I saw Mironov uses quite a lot of found materials (one exhibition of kinetic Rube Goldberg-like sculptures included a room-sized contraption that incorporated everything from hand saws to skis to an old pram). I was bound to ask whether this element is part of his aesthetic or indicates that the flow of normal supplies in tenuous. "Not problem getting what I need", he replied. "I deal with, you know, Soviet robbers." He laughed, but I couldn't tell whether he was joking, for he is a nervously gregarious fellow. Later he played Russian folk songs on his guitar and poured brandies all round and offered slices of what I first took to be a piece of wood, for it looked like a carpenter's leavings, but turned out to be an Armenian meat, spiced within an inch of its life — and of ours.

What impressed me about Mironov's work was not only its range but its range of sincerity. Maybe *intensity* is a better word. His painted wooden figures of contemporary everyman and everywoman, often with right angles redesigning the human form and commenting perhaps on the angularity of big-city existence, struck me as the most deeply felt, followed by some very personal pieces in stone or wood, such as a torso of his wife when she was pregnant with their son, who is now three. But the same person can also commit an enormous plaster bust of Peter the Great, of the sort appropriate to a schoolroom long ago — not as one of his many lucrative commissions but totally self-assigned. The spectrum is so broad, East to West, contemporary to traditional, that it is almost a kind of doubt. He couldn't be more different from Harry Vinogradov, a true underground and decidedly unofficial artist who, for reasons that did not quite survive the translation process, signs himself Bicapo.

He is thirty-two, the same generation as Mironov. His great-grandfather was a famous St. Petersburg mystic and faith-healer, who was sent to Siberia where in 1937 he was killed. Vinogradov/Bicapo carries on some of the same fascination with the idea that madness is sometimes connected to saintliness, a proposition that runs deep in Russian culture. "All people have to do rituals", he said, "to help them to re-establish relations with Nature." His head is shaven, like a penitent's or a prisoner's rather than like a skinhead's, and he affects unusual modes of dress. One day, he recalled, he was wearing a scarf over his head with a hat jammed down over top of that, and a police officer took him to task, saying, "You'll never be another Marc Chagall unless you have a proper smoking suit." The cop didn't know that at that moment Bicapo was naked under his coat.

He studied architecture, found work as a draughtsman but gave it up "because it was an impossibility for one of my temperament — I prefer the status of a free artist." A number of Soviet painters find the term *free artist* useful. It suggests people who are not direct descendants of the old avant-garde of 1910–30, of the Kandinskys, Komardenkovs, and Konstamntinovs who paralleled the modernists in the West, but rather of the artists whose work, in one especially notorious incident, was ordered destroyed by Krushchev in 1962 — an entire group show ground up by bulldozers.

The point is not necessarily that Bicapo works in art forms that the state does not recognize. Not that performance art is exactly a state priority, though the ministry of culture now brags that, in contrast to "the period of stagnation from Stalin to Chernenko", all disciplines may be recognized and rock'n'roll may even be perceived as an official export. Yet people like Bicapo don't receive aid from the cultural arm of the government. Some other apartment artists (so called because they are forced to show their work at open-houses rather than in galleries) have become prosperous through overseas sales — part of the new vogue for Soviet art in the West, a by-product of Gorbamania. "Sometimes the neighbours would call the police when they saw a foreigner come up the steps", Maria said. Bicapo, for his part, was in a group called the Kindergarten Artists, because for a time he and a few friends supported themselves as night guards at a day-care centre and school.

Like two million other Muscovites, Bicapo and his mother share their apartment with another family, or they used to. One fellow tenant has died, two others have moved away. So now he has his studio space next to his living quarters, on the top floor of an apartment building that was built as recently as the 1930s but looks to be covered in at least a century's worth of grime. The lobby smells of urine and the lift is broken; the stairs are lighted only partway up.

The essence of his current work involves the intersection of fire, water, and music. To explain "Bicapo consciousness", he first lit candles around the room and struck a series of chimes he had made by suspending different lengths of steel pipe from the ceiling; the sound lingered and then merged with that of a cassette tape he put on, one track of which consisted of the same chimes while the others were strange sounds I could not identify, half human perhaps and half inorganic, climaxing in what might be screams. All this while two small beer kegs suspended from the ceiling were dripping water into a pair of shallow receptacles that looked like prospector's gold-pans, only larger. Also hanging from above was a circular wire basket in which the artist had put six or eight fuel pellets and ignited them with a blow torch. The heat rising from the basket caused a large aluminium printing plate, slung over a wire as a blanket might be slung over a clothesline, to vibrate. A microphone connected to an amplifier was placed down a two-metre section of plastic flexi-pipe, the sort used for household plumbing, which pipe was dangled from a light chain and tilted, so that one end, the one with the mike, was close to the water pans, which continued to fill up, *drip-drip-drip*. Bicapo then passed the blow torch along the length of the pipe, varying the size of the flame. The sounds picked up by the microphone varied accordingly. Clearly, this is how he made the sounds that I heard on the tape; other tracks — of hammering and sawing, for example — had been mixed in later.

"I first did this with 10 metres of metal tubing at a construction site", Bicapo explained. "I inserted one end of the tube into a fire while a woman sang opera." This was not so much mere street theatre; he is quite earnest about musical structure and the mixing of created and found sound, but his high seriousness is more apparent from his conversation than from his writings on the theory of his art. He allowed me to look at a draft manifesto that described Bicapia as "radiant, equilibristic, superconducting superrapid interaction momentary understanding." But his English orthography slipped in a handbill that he let me take away with me, which declared: "The water is drip, the fire is burn. Losting primordial human natur is manifest when thousands of Bicapo and Dzoings are sound. I am mystacal artist through my madness I am penetrate heavens and listen musik of sky forest."

I wasn't able to determine what Dzoings are.

4
RED ARROW, RED SQUARE

I struck gold on the midnight train to Leningrad.

Like all the other overnight trains, such as those to Helsinki, Vilnius, or other points north and west, this one, called the Red Arrow, has compartments with two berths each, side by side, and I found myself sharing with a woman in her seventies, dressed in a very middle-class manner but with a ratty old cardigan over her suit. On her left lapel she had affixed pins or medals, ones I had never seen in that country of military decorations — both cameos of someone (not Lenin), one black, the other red and black. I asked her what they were, and she told me that they showed her membership in the Soviet Academy of Science and in its Italian equivalent. "I do not usually feel disposed to wear insignia but today was different", she said. She was a retired mathematician, and the occasion was a gathering of the clan in Moscow, from which she was now returning home. She spoke the English of someone who had learned it before the Great Patriotic War — might almost have learned it before the Revolution, the last time that Russia was part of Europe.

How long had she resided in Leningrad?

"It has been my home uninterruptedly since 1947."

Then she had not been there during the war, during the Nazi siege lasting 900 days?

"But I was, yes. I was a young student, and I took very ill. The German circle around the city was complete except for one small opening, and I was evacuated and taken back to Moscow. When I recovered, I continued my studies there."

We talked for many kilometres. She sat perfectly upright; her eyes shone and when she broke into a smile, as she did at every opportunity, the change in her expression took up the slack that the years had given her face, the lower part in particular.

I asked her how she had come to receive the pin from the Italian academy.

"It was given me two years ago, I believe it was, when I travelled there for that purpose. Things were not always as you find them now. There is *liberalisme* in the Chamber of Deputies and throughout the government; it is in the air. But this was not always so", she said, taking advantage of her understatement to smile again. "I was the first woman mathematician to become a member of the Soviet academy." I gathered that her discipline was almost as much a barrier as her gender, and that even after she was elected there were still obstacles to overcome. "Perhaps six years ago the international symposium was held in Montreal, but I was not permitted to go." But with the Gorbachev ascendancy, the mood changed instantly; the trip to Italy was her first and so far only visit to the West.

Finally we grew tired of talking. She put out the lamp, saying merrily, "There is too much illumination in the carriage." We lay back on our respective bunks. Whenever we passed through a town during the night I could see her head silhouetted in the flickering light. It looked as though it belonged on a ancient coin.

As it happened, I saw Leningrad in strict sunshine, which it is possible to do only sixty-five or at most a hundred days of the year. This good luck no doubt contributed to my general impression that Leningrad is on balance one of the handsomest cities I have ever been in. I mean the old central city, which became the capital in 1712, a few years after it was founded, and retained the distinction for 200 years. But even the outer districts, with rusty factories in the Soviet manner, are not without a 1930s late modernist charm. They make you forget for a moment how northern a city Leningrad really is, with its Baltic air and immense skies. When you move beyond the city — and such is the density that you don't have to move very far, considering that there are 5 million residents — you run into forests of white birch.

When leaving Canada I had stuffed a bag with expendable second-hand paperbacks for consumption in queues and waiting rooms (and learned when I arrived that they make welcome gifts as the appetite for English books was hearty everywhere I went). Quite by chance I came upon a passage in *Walden* in which Thoreau enumerates his reasons for choosing to settle at Walden Pond. "No Neva marshes to be filled; though you must everywhere build on piles of your own driving", he writes. "It is said that a flood-tide, with a westerly wind, and ice in the Neva, would sweep St. Petersburg from the face of the earth." But it's not like that at all, at least not in the warmer months. The Neva is a broad river that cuts a deep blue pattern through the heart of the city, augmented by small canals that suggest a miniature (and cleaner) Venice. On both banks of the river, for as far as one can see in both directions, are perfect baroque buildings from the eighteenth century and classical ones from the early part of the nineteenth. Many are painted in pastel shades — not, as in Portugal, say, to show themselves best in direct sunlight but to fight back against the absence of it. The Winter Palace, I was surprised to discover, is wintergreen (a mnemonic device in the making for anyone who has difficulty remembering what buildings were stormed in the Revolution). The low line of harmonious rooftops is interupted here and there by a church spire or a gold dome. One such dome, in the distance, belongs to St Isaac's Cathedral, whose columns still bear some scars from the war. It is located across the square from the Astoria Hotel, which Hitler vowed to make into a museum of the conquest of Leningrad. Some chicken, some neck. The pockmarks on St Isaac's are retained as a reminder, like a sign on a building in Nevsky Prospekt, the principal commercial street, requesting pedestrians to walk on the other side of the avenue during periods of bombardment.

The damage done during the war went beyond what would be suggested by the word extensive; it was heartbreaking. But the Soviets are the world's champion restorers and rebuilders, and neither the antiquarian symmetry of the riverfront nor the open-handed bustle of Nevsky Prospekt, with its often magnificent pre-Revolutionary shops, shows Leningrad for the tragic and violent place it has so often been. Granted that by now there should be no way of recalling that three-quarters of the buildings were destroyed in the war against Napoleon. What is implausible — and it flies in the face of all sensory logic too — is that it is not easy to connect the place with its revolutionary past — Leningrad, where the Decembrists rose up, where the men of the cruiser *Aurora*, which is now a floating museum, fired some of the first shots of the Revolution, where Lenin disembarked at the Finland Station, his exile ended. But it is so. I found it much easier to conceive of Moscow, where intellectual and artistic ferment go together with a gritty workaday existence, as the epicentre of past political earthquakes than Leningrad, which was merely the hub of government, the aristocracy, and the capitalist business culture that were being overthrown. Not that it is remote from the present political turmoil. On the contrary. Only weeks earlier a crowd of 100,000 had gathered outside the Winter Palace to protest the possibility that the two former prosecutors whose stories of corruption had been printed in the *Moscow News* might lose their immunity. I saw graffiti such as "Fucken Police" and the letter A in a circle, the international sign for anarchism. Yet despite all that, Leningrad is definitely the quieter place, with both a deeper level of culture and a sense of inferiority, perhaps equally profound, about having become the second city. The comparisons are inexact enough to be odious, but Leningrad is to Moscow as Montreal is to Toronto, San Francisco is to Los Angeles, and Melbourne is to Sydney.

As befits a city that in czarist times gave pride of place to its magnificent classical Stock Exchange (now a naval museum, but maybe not for much longer), it is also, or so I found, a greedier place than Moscow as regards the poor Soviets' eternal quest for the magical American dollars — greedier and so ruder, because the mission is clear and the time to accomplish it so brief. My experience of Intourist employees I dealt with in Moscow, for example, was that they were uniformly helpful and efficient and usually friendly to boot; but the ones in Leningrad wore *renfrogné* expressions that were matched by their voices. One or two of the foreigners' hotels in Moscow have a few discreet slot machines in the lobby to extract yet a few more dollars or pounds per year, but in Leningrad they are more numerous and not at all hidden; in one instance, there is a sort of miniature casino, gaudily lit. Maybe that kind of thing is to be expected in any city whose museums and treasures make it a place where tourism is disproportionately important to the economy (20,000 people per day visit the Hermitage museum, 40,000 per day in the summer and during holidays). One incident for me crystallized Leningrad's position in this matter.

Wherever I went, I found, as so many western visitors do, that people were forever approaching me to change dollars into rubles at the best black market *valuta* (you would have to be crazy to run the risk of accepting) or to try to sell me wristwatches or vodka. Leningrad exceeded all the boundaries. Spotting me as a foreigner (it is my fate always to look like a foreigner wherever I am, even when I stay home), young men would enquire in whispers whether I might wish Soviet flags or icons or caviar (three jars for $10 — "special price"). The most original was a chap not far from the main entrance of the Admiralty. He was in civilian attire but I took him to be a sailor by his distinctive haircut — and because Leningrad has been full of sailors since it was established originally to be the country's western seaport. He was carrying a bag of some rough cloth, bigger than a large pillow-slip. I thought I saw it move, leading me to suppose that it contained a chicken or perhaps a litter of kittens. But what he wanted was to sell his — or somebody's — dress uniform, complete with braided cap and epaulets. I declined, and we each scurried off in stoic embarrassment like two people whose stomachs had been rumbling in public. Naval discipline, I gathered, is not what it once was.

I stayed in Leningrad a couple of days, looking at paintings and buildings and talking to as many people as I could, including bathers sunning themselves on the sand beneath the walls of Peter and Paul Fortress, the old political prison. I marvelled at the brevity of their costume, given that I found it cold enough to warrant something midway between a mackintosh and an overcoat. They're a hardy mob, those Leningraders.

I wish I could report that my return journey to Moscow was as rewarding as the trip up had been, but it was merely memorable. My roommate this time was a merchant seaman who kept addressing me as *Englander*. I had all the more reason to not split hairs, but simply accept this as the generous compliment it was, given that he was as drunk as a — well, as a sailor. He couldn't move more than a few steps without banging his head into something, and he kept dropping the sheaf of roses that he told me were for his wife in Moscow. He also confessed, rather needlessly, that he had been out with his friends and had consumed quite a lot of vodka. He told me that he knew my country well, and rhymed off the landmarks: Tilbury Docks, Tower Bridge, Big Ben. . . . By the end of the list he was singing rather than reciting them.

I confessed my fatigue and asked whether I might put out the light. But when I did he would simply turn it on again. And my plan of going to the Soviet Union with the intention of ignoring my own shyness and talking with as many different citizens as possible was put to the test by the fact that, after an hour or so, I still couldn't get him to shut the bloody hell up. So I was relieved when he announced that he was leaving our compartment in search of more vodka. When he found some, though, he returned to shake me awake and insist that I share it with him. I sent him away and fell asleep again. He then sent as an emissary to reawaken me the woman whose vodka it was. I told her to get out. Some while later the sailor barged back into the room to retrieve his wife's roses, presumably for redistribution amongst women elsewhere in the carriage. That must have been at 3 a.m. or so. When we pulled into the station at seven he was asleep, slouched over like a big sack of onions, snoring a deafening snore. I left him there and went in search of a taxi driver I could bribe.

For all the reverence I saw in people's behaviour at the Lenin Mausoleum, I also heard, throughout my stay, a lot of condemnation of his shade or maybe of the Lenin cult. Much of it was expressed at the level of satire or humour, however seriously it was felt. One person told me that in his lifetime he had seen fifty coats or suits of clothes that once belonged to Lenin hanging in various museums — "and they're all of different sizes." At another exhibit I heard a woman argue quite seriously and cogently that Leningrad should be given back its old name; this surprised me, but soon a powerful movement would spring up around this idea. But of Stalin who betrayed the Revolution and commenced not only the Era of Stagnation but the long reign of terror, I heard much less derision. I couldn't quite tell to what extent this was because his statue had been kicked over long ago and to what extent it was because the plinth was still warm. Maybe hatred of Stalin is simply taken for granted. Taking a poke at Lenin was certainly a different matter, a safe novelty, part of the new freedom, the changes in change itself, the liberal counter-revolution.

The joyous assumptions of Americans to the contrary, this new revolution is not necessarily a purblind rush to embrace America or the right. No one is advocating turning the U.S.S.R. into another U.S.A.; surely Gorbachev, faced with a deepening national emergency, is simply making socialism far more flexible, as Franklin Roosevelt, when in a similar corner, made capitalism more flexible. The point isn't the cold war except to the extent that the Cold War is too expensive for either side to continue fighting, most of all the Soviets, who have a standing army of 4 million but, according to the more liberal military planners at defence headquarters across the river from Gorky Park, need a mere

1.7 million. It is simply about moving nearer the middle, with more democracy and a more mixed economy than in the past, trying to improve the lot of individuals (and preserving the power of those now bringing about the improvements). Yet the changes are abrupt. They could still turn out to be violent. Certainly they will cause some aspects of Soviet life to worsen before they improve. This much was brought home to me again and again as I spoke with people about their fears and aspirations.

It is obvious to the least observant visitor that the present system guarantees full employment only by perpetuating a ridiculous level of over-staffing. Four people work in a cloakroom that might be handled by one. To buy a plane ticket or rent a hotel room or get a loaf of bread in a bakery, you are passed from person to person, each of whom undertakes some further perfunctory part of the process. A retail purchase that in a state-run shop in China might require the services of two or three persons could easily, in the Soviet Union, take those of four or five — one to show you where the item is, a second to fetch it down, another to take your money, yet another to take your receipt and do the wrapping. As the old socialist jest has it, "We pretend to work and they pretend to pay us." There is an important difference between this arrangement in the U.S.S.R. and the impression I got in China that the government was at least making the best use of its most obvious asset — the labour force. That it is difficult to feel the same about the Soviets is no doubt coloured by the way the country is routinely rumoured to be on the brink of collapse — an ethnocentric western view, I feel, since we have no real understanding of how long it has been as bad as it is and no way to measure the Russians' extraordinary capacity for swallowing adversity and making the best of chaos.

This is the difficulty in trying to interpret events in the socialist world at present: the Americans refuse to believe anything good about the Soviets, that the people are generally better educated, less violent, and leading perhaps altogether deeper lives than they themselves are, whereas the Soviets, or the young ones ar least, refuse to believe anything bad about the West — the drugs, the crime, the homelessness, the AIDS. A general lack of attention to reality obscures the simple truth that the quality of life in the one place is improving and in the other place deteriorating but that, in any event, they are becoming more alike.

I was told that it wouldn't be long now before Soviet citizens would be free to possess credit cards — despite the absence, so far, of all the necessary mainframes and software. One can only imagine what a mess might result, given that virtually every place of business in the country still uses the abacus in preference to the cash register. They have cash registers, all right, but they don't use them for any form of tabulation but merely as places to keep large-denomination notes, as one might use a microwave oven as a bookcase. In that environment, the moves towards a market economy are bound to be painful. People may cheer when bureaucrats are put out of work, but what about when they themselves must go and living standards plummet? As it stands, 45 million Soviets live on 70 rubles a month. In Moscow alone, there are 1.7 million people below the official poverty line, and when I was there the new mayor announced plans for municipally funded soup kitchens. By the time they are open, it is expected that the price of most consumer goods will have risen 100 per cent. No one disputes that such changes are necessary or that the existing social net must be remade, but with new measurements to protect pensioners and others on fixed incomes, if the country is to stabilize its currency. Stabilizing it is the first step towards internationalizing it. At present, the much-vaunted joint ventures between Soviets and western businesspeople, about 1,300 of them at this writing, don't work because the westerners don't want to be paid in worthless rubles and there are not enough dollars or Deutschmarks for the purpose. The joint ventures are necessary, however, to improve the supply and quality of consumer goods. To an extent I was prepared to accept but couldn't quite fathom until I saw the situation with my own eyes, the problem of the Soviet Union is the problem of food. No one actually starves to death, as of old, but Gorbachev must be aware all too acutely of a rule that has cautioned leaders for thousands of years, that hungry people are dangerous people.

Then there are social ills we don't usually see, for a variety of reasons. There is indeed a slight drug problem in the U.S.S.R., though hardly on the scale of any western European country. One of the reasons you hear so little about it is that it does not involve smuggling and international borders, for the drugs come from areas of the country close to Afghanistan (though intelligence specialists have long insisted that China illicitly supplies drugs to its old adversary, just as it is supposed to have flooded the Vietnamese market twenty-five years ago to help demoralize the American troops). Crime is rising in the big cities, as it is in big cities everywhere, I suppose. There are places in Moscow, just as in the West, where for fear of rape women are afraid to enter their own apartment buildings alone after dark. I saw beggars in the subway underpasses, but not many; so far there is virtually no homelessness as such, though the extent and quality of housing is a pressing problem and a major subject of anxiety — but having said so, there is no point getting sucked into any East–West comparisons when the systems are so fundamentally different.

By contrast, the whole range of women's issues is a useful illustration of the similarities and differences. "There is no feminist movement", a teacher in her forties explained to me. "We have equal pay for equal work, and women do about all the jobs that men do." There is, however, a "women's lobby", which is expected to challenge the spread of such complacency and to address imbalances, such as that only 8 per cent of political offices in the Soviet Union are held by women (as compared, for example, with the Commons in Ottawa, where 13.5 per cent of the MPs are women — hardly a figure to justify smugness). Perhaps the harshest fact of women's existence is that though both partners must work, the woman must still perform all the domestic functions previously expected of her, and moreover that this presents even greater difficulty than in the West. The father does not usually take part in child care. It is also the woman who spends two or three hours shopping for food for the night's supper (only to find sometimes, after getting to the head of the line, that the food is spoiled). Women are not *social* equals. What was called male chauvinism in the West in the 1970s is the common currency in the Soviet Union, though there is no name for it and it is almost completely unremarked on by either gender so far as public discussion goes; it is simply part of the culture. If lucky enough to be invited into a private home, the western visitor may be shocked by how the husband denigrates his wife's domestic skills as a means of apologizing, needlessly of course, for the lack of what they imagine to be western comfort. No wonder that 33 per cent of marriages end in divorce, which accounts for 70 per cent of all activity in the courts; in more than 98 per cent of divorce cases involving children, the mother is given custody. The parting couple must pay a 300-ruble divorce tax (until recently 200 rubles — inflation again). Child support payments are generous, but of course that never really solves the problem. The nation may now be self-sufficient in blue jeans, much to the impoverishment of black marketeers and shrewd western tourists. What it lacks so conspicuously are condoms, which, when available at all, are of unreliable quality. I was told that for western visitors to give their host or hostess condoms would not be misunderstood but, on the contrary, would seem considerate. Abortion may be free on demand, but it is virtually the only form of birth control worthy of the name. Fully 20 per cent of first pregnancies end in abortion.

Alcoholism is another factor in marriage break-down as it is in poor work productivity. One of Gorbachev's first initiatives was the major campaign against alcohol abuse, even to the extent of banning the sale of hard liquor (but not its consumption) on trains and planes. Reaction against the "authoritarian" campaign was among the causes that enabled Yeltsin to get his political comeback underway. One senses that economic loss, not health, is the primary concern, given that virtually no acknowledgement is made of the fact that 78 per cent of adult males and 38 per cent of adult females smoke cigarettes. The U.S.S.R. is in fact a nation of inveterate chainsmokers. "Sure, we have free housing, or virtually free", I was told. One person I talked to paid just 17 rubles a month for an apartment in downtown Moscow, a tiny portion of his middle-class salary. "But the quality is poor. With health care, it is similar. It is free of charge, and available to everyone, but the quality I believe you would call lousy." I heard stories, which I was not able to confirm, of a drug shortage so severe that patients in polyclinics have died from infection after routine operations such as appendectomies. People want change to come and soon, sooner than may be possible, in fact. The good thing about the present, after all, is that there are no surprises.

Kropotkin Street, named to honour the great anarchist, was formerly known as Blessed Virgin Street. It contains a sinister building partly hidden by a high wall topped with barbed wire; this is one of the psychiatric institutions where dissidents were held against their will and, in a few cases, still are, if rumours are correct. A short distance along is a building that was long home to two elderly women who kept scores of cats. Five years ago, however, the cats were removed, the house became Moscow's first co-operative, which is to say free-enterprise, restaurant, known simply as No. 36 Kropotkin. It won't even accept dollars much less rubles but takes only credit cards and is frequented by groups of foreigners or by single foreigners like me, eager to repay the genuine hospitality of some Soviet acquaintances. It is not the most expensive of the seven or eight such eating-places in the city; I was advised in a hushed tone that at a Chinese restaurant called the Peking the shark's fin soup costs 100 rubles. But it is representative, I believe, and symbolic.

Eating in any Soviet restaurant, you are conscious first of all that the printed menu, considered as literature and as theatre, serves quite a different function than in the West. In our tradition, the menu is a basic list. You expect the waiter to ooze over to the table and say something like, "Good evening, my name is Mark, and I'll be your server this evening. In addition to our menu selections, chef has prepared the following specials. . . ." Soviet menus by comparison are little encyclopaedias, page after page of every conceivable chicken dish, fish dish, vegetable dish. The job of the server is to explain, in response to your enquiries, that the dishes you want are not available — until you begin to suspect that they have never been available. "So what, then, do you suggest this evening?" you are finally forced to ask.

"Bifsteak." Boiled beef.

"What would you recommend to go with that?"

"Cabbage."

"Is anything else available?"

"Cabbage."

A cold fish course comes first; the meat is the second course and is always boiled. Fresh fruit and vegetables are almost nonexistent. No. 36 was offering carrots that night, but they were cold. It was amusing to see the head waiter in evening clothes and the junior staff in stiff white tunics, trying to suggest the pre-Revolutionary style. They had the snooty looks down pat but kept serving and taking away from the wrong sides. The example may be a small one but the point is bigger: one of the reasons why individual entrepreneurship is far more widespread and obviously more successful in China than in the Soviet Union, I heard it said, is that in China there is still an old generation that remembers how the salary system works; 1917 is just that much longer ago than 1949 to make the same continuity impossible in the U.S.S.R.

Outside in the streets, however, the world before the Revolution is apparent enough, in the old apartment blocks, the former private houses, the hotels or public buildings that serve completely different functions now but are so clearly a part of their own time and place — and class. Even the arrangement of the streets and boulevards shows the wealth that once obtained there. It is like London in that respect, though in general the similarity to the United States seems more pressing and germane: another of those sprawling, powerful, ungovernable countries that can proceed only by lurching from extreme to extreme in a kind of slow-motion ricochet in which innocent people so often get hurt.

I managed to wangle a VIP pass to the May Day parade in Red Square, but was told to bring my passport and visa (the latter is a separate document, not something stamped in the former). Security promised to be tight because this was not an ordinary May Day, or Day of the International Solidarity of the Working People, to give it its full official name. For one thing, it was the one-hundredth consecutive May Day parade to be held in Red Square. Some will be surprised to learn that this is a pre-Revolutionary holiday in new red clothes. It is in fact a pre-Christian celebration of the return of spring; even some of the Russian songs associated with it may date back the better part of a millennium. Some elements of the original ceremony survived into the era when aging patriarchs standing side by side atop the Lenin Mausoleum would give feeble geriatric waves at the endless line of troops and missile-carriers passing below. That is the May Day we in the West know from years of television clips, though in fact the displays of unending might have always been much more important as a feature of Victory Day on May 9.

In any case, this year it was to be very different. No military parade at all and no rogues gallery of Red Army generals to take the salute — that would have been too Stalinist in tone and, in the present atmosphere, too provocative. This time the various trade unions and such would do the marching, organized not by the government but by the Society of Moscow Voters, a pro-reform organization, and others, but with the approval of the Council of Ministers, which also gave permission for a demonstration — a manifestation, as the Soviets say — to be held around the corner, so to speak, in Revolution Square. I couldn't find anyone who knew for certain whether Gorbachev himself would turn up. In Leningrad and other cities, the holiday would be marked in similarly radical ways; in Kiev, local people did without government representation in the reviewing stand altogether.

By nine-thirty or so the area around the Kremlin was filling up with humanity. I heard the size of the crowd estimated variously at 100,000 and 300,000 — the latter seemed too high to me, but it makes no difference really. I kept track of the number of times my papers were scrutinized at different checkpoints as I got closer to Lenin's tomb; the final tally was nine. The soldiers were being equally careful with diplomats, I noticed. From the cement steps where I perched, closer to the reviewing stand, downwind, than to the Historical Museum to my left, where the marchers would proceed from, I had a fine view of the goings-on. I could see columns mustering, banners being unfurled and tested, brightly coloured groups of walkers pacing like horses impatient for the race to begin. To the right, TV camera crews on an unstable-looking scaffold were training their equipment on the top of the mausoleum, where the new extra-military dignitaries would stand. Soldiers were everywhere. There were also many security men in black leather trenchcoats with walkie-talkies. Through the long lens of my camera I could see others directly ahead, across the great cobblestone square, positioned along the rooftops.

I moved my gaze downward and began scanning faces in the crowd through my view-finder. During one pan I stopped with a jolt of recognition. The face was unmistakable. Yes, it was Honest Ed Mirvish, the zillionaire proprietor of Toronto's oldest, largest, and altogether most garish discount store, a man who had parlayed the nine-cent lightbulb and the job lot of slightly imperfect ladies' ready-to-wear into a famous dynastic fortune. He was wearing a beautifully tailored dark blue wool suit and handmade Italian shoes that shone like obsidian. He seemed to be giving some people his business card. For just a moment, before he was swallowed by the crowd, I saw him framed against the GUM Department Store and could imagine it as perhaps he might hope to see it, its 2.4 kilometres of counter space brimming with toilet rolls and polyester tank tops, its long facade plastered in neon and witty sayings and blow-ups of articles from the Toronto *Telegram* extolling the legend of Honest Ed (boy, what a card). I couldn't help but wonder whether he knew the significance of what he was about to see or whether it reminded him of the Eaton's Santa Claus parades when he was a kid.

At the stroke of ten, band music came over the public address system, followed by short speeches from a series of sonorous, disembodied voices. The first speech was booed but not consistently or with real persistence. By now I could see the thin line of figures on the reviewing stand. The pent-up marchers were released, and there was another flurry of brass and drums, but live this time, from somewhere within the multitude. The participants lunged forward, men in suits, women in dresses, lots of children, some holding red flowers straight out front like votive offerings. Suddenly I realized what a sea of colour it was, how surprised I was to see all the bright fabrics together, for after even so short a time in the country my eyes had become accustomed to the more limited spectrum that is certainly one of the features of existence there, quite apart from any quality-of-life considerations.

The parade went on. Then it went on some more, and some more. My vantage point was privileged, but I realized that it was also constricted; I couldn't see Gorbachev from where I was, I couldn't even see whether he had turned up. There were gasps now at the wording on some of the placards and banners bobbing over the heads of the crowd. I asked someone to translate. One read "The Communist Party of the Soviet Union Exploits Us". Another ran: "GET OUT OF OUR POCKETS NOW!" I felt compelled to see how the fellows on the reviewing stand were reacting. I needed to move to the east, but whenever I tried I was stopped by the militia police or by the plain-clothes security. For the same reasons it seemed hopeless to try to make a circuitous route, westward to the museum at the edge of the square and then along 25th October Street, through the back door, as it were; that would have put the whole crowd between me and the mausoleum and I wasn't certain I would find a sufficiently elevated spot there such as the one I already enjoyed where I was. The only thing to do was to join the parade and become one of the marchers myself. If anyone tried to prevent me from doing so I would make a fuss and insist that I was one of the cultural workers (for such is how my editor must think of me, I said to myself).

An organization of machinists was going past. I could identify them by the logotype of meshing gears on their signboards. I stepped down and slipped sideways between the guards and was swept up in the marchers before anyone could stop me. We hadn't gone many metres before I caught sight of Gorbachev. He was the twelfth from the right, in his trademark topcoat and little grey hat. His wool scarf had an irregular pattern of red in it, no doubt in honour of the occasion. He was looking impassive and occasionally he waved in somewhat the same way we associate with the Queen. I got to look at him only for half a minute before the momentum of the crowd pushed me and my fellow machinists along. I didn't see any obvious concern on his face, but my intuition, I believe, was correct. Shortly afterward, thanks partly to an administrative mix-up, the demonstration in Revolution Square was permitted to tag on to the end of our parade, not far behind me, and when these other marchers reached the vicinity of the reviewing stand, they produced loud-hailers and began shouting personal insults at the president, who lost his patience and walked off.

The next day, this incident was the talk of the town, though the media were cautious at first, referring only to evidence of displeasure in the parade and in the unofficial demonstration. Radio Moscow merely referred to some slogans of "an explicit and controversial nature" that would have been unthinkable at any time in the past. But gradually, as time went on and the various weeklies appeared, the story came out a few details at a time, to the point where *Moskovskaya Pravda*, as the local edition is called, one day ran a front-page interview with the first secretary of the party. It was headed "On the Wave of Irresponsibility".

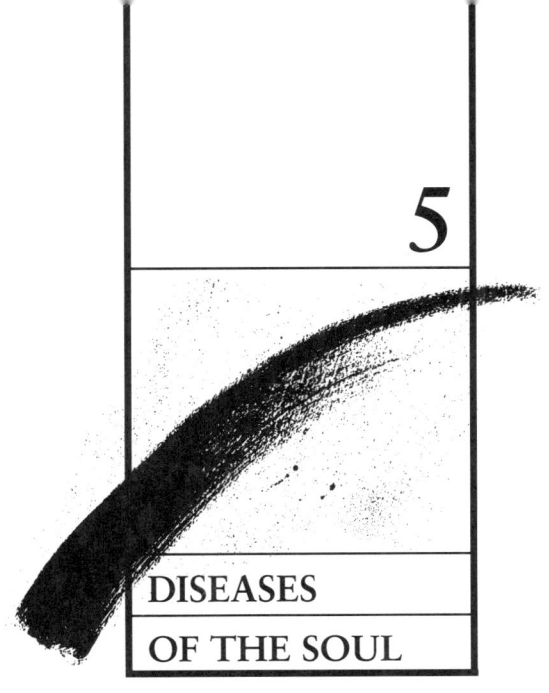

5

DISEASES OF THE SOUL

There are naturally two museums in central Moscow devoted to Maxim Gorky. One of them is the house where he spent his last few years and wrote his last books. It was there that he died — murdered by his doctors, some say. The story is that they were acting on orders from Stalin, who apparently feared that Gorky was becoming too much of a folk hero. Others believe that Stalin personally killed him, by giving him poisoned candy. How many Soviet biographies end this way — "murdered by Stalin"? — though the motive was not usually jealousy.

What makes the Gorky house truly interesting is not the memorabilia displayed there but the structure itself, which dates to about 1900. It was confiscated from the person who built it, a manufacturer and banker named Ryabushinsky. He was a great patron of the modern artists, whom he commissioned to design stained-glass windows and balustrades and every other sort of decorative component. The result suggests what might have come about if Roger Fry and his Omega Workshop had been given carte blanche to create a total environment. Something about the front entrance struck me immediately. There are large brass hinges on the thick double doors. I couldn't be certain, for the design is somewhat stylized, but it certainly seemed to me that the hinges were meant to represent a menorah. I remember this detail because it is impossible to conceive of anyone in Moscow since the turn of the century who would have been brave enough, or foolhardy enough, to flaunt his or her Jewishness in quite that way. Certainly no one would do so today. The Soviet Union, unfortunately, seems a very anti-Semitic place. The evidence suggests that it has always been so, of course, but the new mood of relative freedom has permitted the old animosities to be expressed publicly.

In the couple of months before I arrived in the country, anti-Semitism appeared to be breaking out everywhere, from Irkutsk in Siberia, where there were outcries about the number of Jews supposedly holding scientific appointments, to Baku in Azerbaijan, where Muslims not ethnic Russians are the persecutors of the 20,000 local Jews, to Odessa on the Black Sea, where the authorities had to issue reminders that inciting racial hatred is a crime. In general, the new wave of anti-Semitism is bound up with the politics of Russian nationalism. One of the main instigators is Pamyat (the word means memory), an ultra-rightist group based in Moscow and Leningrad. It has called for keeping Jews out of teaching jobs, doctoral programmes, local governments, and even the CPSU. When I was there, rumours about a pogrom — that was the word being used — in Leningrad on May 5 were gaining currency. Fortunately they were just rumours, but they had been circulated with a certain desired effect. Officially, there are only about 1.5 million Jews in the Soviet Union, because many went to pains to disguise or submerge their Jewishness during the Stalin years and later. The true figure is at least 50 per cent greater and may be twice as large; the heaviest concentration is in Moscow, about 200,000.

A majority of Soviet Jews are intending to emigrate to Israel. This year for the first time Passover was proudly covered on Soviet television, and I saw posters announcing exhibits of Jewish art and Jewish history. Yet such activity carries a suggestion that the culture it represents is passing from the Soviet scene, though at this time Gorbachev was threatening to keep the Jews from leaving unless Israel undertook not to settle them on the occupied West Bank and Gaza Strip (a demand it eventually agreed to). In any event, the new religious freedom being granted the Christians has resulted only in more anti-Semitism. That China has no noticeable anti-Semitism has less to do with the fact that it has only a handful of Jews than with the fact that it has so little political freedom. (Buddhism there is mostly for show. In Tibet, for example, there were 106,000 priests and 2,400 monasteries as late as 1960, after the refugees had left. Today there are 2,000 priests at most and only 10 monasteries. The most important feature of religious freedom, perhaps, is that it needs political freedom in order to flourish.)

Another hotbed of anti-Semitism in the Soviet Union — though also of reaction against it — is the literary community, in particular the Writers' Union of the Russian Republic, where there have been actual fistfights over the issue. Only a very few writers, such as Stanislav Kunyaev, are anti-Semitic agitators, but they have a disruptive effect, and as I learned one evening over dinner in the union's dining room, the polarization extends deep into the profession. I was with two young people, both junior editors. They were well educated, not at all susceptible to the crude canards of the Protocols of the Elders of Zion, which the czars and Hitler used to fan hatred of Jews and which various groups in the provinces are once again spreading about as "proof" of a worldwide Jewish conspiracy. Nonetheless, they were quite firm in what they did believe.

"Most of the leaders of the Revolution were Jews", one of the editors told me. Well, some were, of course, but the significance of that fact is that the Revolution was hatched by intellectuals as a revolution of ideas. "They planted the seeds for the Soviet system, and you see what condition the Soviet system is in." He was deadly serious about this syllogism and expected others to take it seriously as well: the food shortages were the Jews' fault! I was appalled. This was the view of the Pamyat leaders like Dmitry Vasiliev, though the person across the table from me was hardly a Pamyat type. The other young editor was of the contrary opinion and announced that he was prepared to hide Jews in his home when the situation came to that. Both positions were proclaimed with feverish emotion. Even the person taking the second position, however, kept using the phrase "the Jewish problem", a term that made my blood run cold. I believe that was my second scariest moment in the Soviet Union. The scariest was when a moderate liberal democrat told me, "There are only perhaps four million of us right now who believe as I do. Now people are speaking out, but the door could close on us at any time. Stalin killed how many? Ten million? Twenty million? Gorbachev could kill four million and it wouldn't make a particularly large grave." In fairness to him, my informant was drunk at the time. The young people discussing "the Jewish problem" were deadly sober.

I was relieved to see that the *Literaturnaya Gazeta* came out forcefully in support whenever the government brandished the anti-hate laws against the most blatant offenders, but the whole subject left me worried and weak-kneed. As economic conditions worsen, as they are bound to do before they begin to improve, the anti-Semitism will worsen as well, even though, like so much of the present turmoil, its basis is less in matters of money than in ones of race. When I was there, three of the Baltic republics and three Muslim ones were engaged in plotting to break away from the federal union, and since that time, with Yeltsin's election, the opposite possibility has started to be talked about openly — the possibility of the centre breaking away from the edges.

By a vivid coincidence, the period covered by my trip saw news about census-taking in the United States, China, and the Soviet Union. The U.S. census turned into a shambles of inaccuracy, because there was no effective way, it seems, of enumerating all the transients, bag ladies and other homeless people, winos, junkies, and illegal aliens. China announced that it would begin a thorough new census of the country, a daunting task involving 6 million enumerators to count an estimated 1.1 billion people, and one that immediately aroused suspicions that the operation would be a cover for new means of tightening the grip of authority. In the Soviet Union, by contrast, there were stories about why the census undertaken the previous year had yet to be released and perhaps never would be. The reason, it was supposed, is that results showed the number of Soviet Muslims up by 33 per cent while the number of ethnic Russians had increased by only 5.6 per cent. The whole question is enormously complicated and fraught with great emotion.

In the same room where I eavesdropped on the discussion of anti-Semitism I later had dinner with Igor Shkliarevsky, who is acknowledged to be one of the country's four or five most important poets. He is popular as well as important, so popular, in fact, that the sales of his books provide him with an independent income, which has freed him from much of the cliquishness of Soviet literary life. In recent years he has acquired additional renown as an ecological activist. His interest in the environment has been with him all his life. One of his poems speaks of Canada, which he has never visited, as the "beloved country of my childhood". He of course meant a sort of metaphorical Canada of clean rivers and clear skies; when I disabused him of the image, he was not surprised, for he is not a utopian. Quite the opposite. He has no use for green politics. "No politics", he said. "Everyone now likes to get into politics. There was a plenary session [on the environment] in Moscow city council recently. Nothing but speakers! Not one bird or tree is better for such talk. I'm sick and tired of it." His approach, rather, is the familiar one of individual responsibility, with people tending first to conditions "within their own region, their own state, and their own persona", combined with a massive educational effort to turn out graduates in "new trades such as ecological engineering and such others as will be needed in large numbers before long. Not that we lack ecologists already." He uses the word *ecologists* with a note of disdain, to express the view that they are too concerned with theory. With the accident at Chernobyl, he seemed to be saying, the time for theory ended and the time for treatment of shock and trauma began.

Thanks partly to the exposés of the *Moscow News*, it is now known, or at least argued convincingly, that the amount of radiation let loose when the Chernobyl power station burned in April 1986 was more that twenty times greater than the authorities admitted back then — and that the same authorities not only knew beforehand that the reactor's design was unsafe but failed, after the fact, to evacuate all the people who were in danger. The accident took place on April 26. But five days later, in nearby Kiev, a city of 2.6 million people, the annual May Day celebration was allowed to proceed as usual, though radiation levels had risen to 100 times what was considered safe. According to the *News*, it was only the day after the big parade that a decision was made to evacuate the town of Chernobyl, 14 kilometres from the reactor — and little more that a month before the scheme was completed. Eventually, 25,000 people were removed to the 175 resettlement villages built for that purpose, and it was not long before a 30-kilometre area around the plant was sealed off with concrete and wire, punctuated by armed checkpoints. At least a thousand people who lived in what is now called the Dead Zone found adjustment to their new homes so difficult that they sneaked back, hoping to carry on life as it had been, in their telling phrase, "before the war". The authorities first re-expelled them. Later, the people were permitted to pursue this form of slow suicide, given that most of them are elderly.

Only now are all the medical consequences of the tragedy becoming known: 1.4 million adults and 600,000 children have been contaminated by cesium-137, strontium-90, plutonium-239, and other radioactive isotopes. They either require immediate treatment or will need it sooner or later, for leukosis and a long list of other diseases, spanning the range from anaemia to respiratory and gastroenteric problems to immune disorders and psychological difficulties. Thyroid complaints are particularly common. Deformities in newborn infants and farm animals are frequent.

The political implications can hardly be divorced from the medical ones, yet they are of freestanding significance. Chernobyl seems to have given new force to dissent in the Ukraine, the second largest of the republics, supplying a quarter of the U.S.S.R.'s food and conducting a third of its industry, yet the one where Stalinism and the Stalinist aesthetic lingered longest. There are four large nationalist movements, one of them led by the poet Ivan Drach. They espouse an array of causes, some of them having to do with the Ukrainian language, others centring on the Ukrainian

Catholic Church. But environmental concerns are not very far from most peoples' minds, no matter what the nominal agenda. Forty per cent of the U.S.S.R.'s nuclear reactors are in the Ukraine, and one separatist group claims to know of a secret government plan to build another twenty-seven there by the year 2005. True or not, the story adds to an already well founded fear.

An estimated 70 per cent of the land contaminated by the Chernobyl accident lies not in the Ukraine but in Byelorussia, the neighbouring republic that is home to 10.2 million people, a quarter of them fourteen years old or younger. Even in Minsk, the capital, which received the smallest dose of any city in the region, there have recently been huge demonstrations, complete with black flags and the tolling of funeral bells. Many people in Byelorussia should be going abroad for treatment but lack the hard currency to do so, for it is an especially poor place, without even the money for all the clean-up work that needs to be done. Some citizens are urging that Minsk stop contributing to the Soviet budget until the situation changes. Meanwhile, the republic has appealed to the rest of the world for help in moving 10 million people from twenty-seven cities and 2,600 villages. The response has been shamefully lackadaisical.

Writers, such as Oles Honchar in the Ukraine, have taken a considerable role in this combination of nationalism and environmental activism, but none more so than Shkliarevsky perhaps. By the end of summer 1986 he had visited the danger area, up to the limit of the barriers, 30 kilometres from the reactor. "When I got back I got rid of my clothes, shoes, everything. I had a throat infection. I still cough today." Since then, his pen has not been still on the subject, and he has added his purse to the battle. When he received one of the country's largest literary prizes, 10,000 rubles, he gave away the money to plant 30 hectares of trees, half in Byelorussia, half in the Ukraine. It was a lot of money — especially when you consider "that the fine for polluting rivers is only 500 rubles."

He fears that more than a way of life is being lost, that some part of the soul is dying, not only around Chernobyl but across the face of the country, and has been doing so for a long time. "I first went to Siberia, for instance, in 1959, as a Young Pioneer. I was sent to near Vladivostok. I then went back in 1963. Superficially, conditions were improved, but I was unnerved my first day to find out that a particular type of big fish the people used to love eating was no longer caught. Soon the people forgot how to fish. In the Ukraine and Byelorussia, people for hundreds of years have been gathering mushrooms and strawberries in the forest, and tending their gardens, and doing some fishing in small lakes and rivers. Such activity is strictly forbidden now. Life in the small cities is dead, shops are empty. People are on rafts in an ocean of disaster. There has been some psychological shift in human consciousness, some loss of life-recognition. The sparks of consciousness disappear if you look beneath people's skulls."

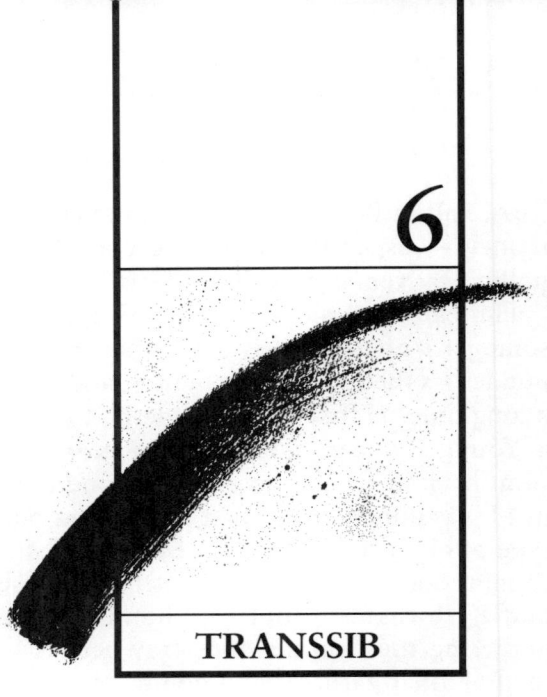

6

TRANSSIB

For the past couple of weeks I hadn't slept more than three or four hours at a stretch. Such rest as I did get took place mostly on a blanket on the floor, because I had sprained my back. The poor diet was beginning to wear me down as well, and the malaria prophylaxis I had begun to take in anticipation of Southeast Asia had started to affect my vision, or so I imagined. More than anything, I suppose, I was talked out, and I looked forward to what I fancied would be the comparative silence of the long train trip through Siberia. I arrived at the station at one in the morning and joined the eager crowd of fellow masochists already assembled there. One was a German wearing a backpack from which a police truncheon protruded. A light rain was falling. It made a high-pitched sound, like Japanese women giggling.

The Trans-Siberian, which the Soviets know as the Rossiya and the Germans call the Transsib, was built in stages between 1891 and 1916, as a matter of economic policy, to open up the barren fastnesses. Until that time, people went overland by *troika*, wrapped up in bearskins in winter, stopping at log post-houses every 40 kilometres. The railway has always had a military and geopolitical purpose as well. On another level, as a national achievement, it was inspired by the Canadian Pacific, though the engineering problems were quite different. One of the project's prime movers was Count Nikolai Ignatieff, a czarist minister and the great-grandfather of Michael Ignatieff, the Canadian man of letters. A complete route map, taking in the later additions, some as recent as the 1950s, is a complicated affair. Basically the idea is to dip southeasterly from Moscow, climb over the Ural Mountains and maintain a more or less straight course across the enormous back of lower Siberia as far as Lake Baikal (where in the early days the railway carriages were transferred to barge-ferries). After that, one line goes northeast to Khabarovsk, where connections can be made to a passenger ferry that plies to Yokohama across the Sea of Japan, while another line cuts sharply south to Mongolia. The terminus of both lines is Beijing, following a passage through Manchuria from one direction or the other. I had bought a ticket that skirted Mongolia, to avoid the necessity of fighting for a Mongolian visa at the Mongol embassy in Moscow, and would be deposited at the Chinese capital via Harbin. I was to travel hard class rather than soft. I wasn't being stoic or going native. I was told that nothing else was available.

There is an extensive literature about the Trans-Siberian, by people as different as the pianist Artur Rubinstein, who crossed in the 1920s, and Laurens van der Post, who made the trip in the 1960s. Two of the seminal British travel writers of the 1930s, Robert Byron and Peter Fleming, described their own journeys in memorable terms. As for contemporaries, Paul Theroux has written on the subject more than once, beginning with *The Great Railway Bazaar* and continuing in *Riding the Iron Rooster*. The latter episode is apparently the one he also deals with in his novel *My Secret History*, and I prefer the fictional version as being truer and less marked by his usual rancour and dislike of foreigners. There are views from the side of the track as well: Yevgeny Yevtushenko grew up in Siberia and writes about the train hurtling through his childhood. Altogether there is enough to make an attractive little anthology, sufficient for whiling away another couple of hours on a ride that seems, towards the end especially, as though it will never end, what with the nature of the accommodations and the nature of the landscape and the curious way they interact.

Before the Revolution the train had grand pianos and marble bathtubs. No more. But then it is not really designed for tourists, though tourists take it in increasing numbers — to the extent that Siberian prostitutes seeking dollars or marks are said to have begun boarding the train at one isolated station, plying their trade for a while, then disembarking at another God-forsaken whistle stop farther down the line. I saw none of this particular brand of *perestroika*, perhaps because I was on the so-called express, which makes only short pauses at some of the largest towns and cities.

Like the BAM line in eastern Siberia, which runs parallel some distance to the north but is off-limits to foreigners because of its military connotations, the Trans-Siberian is the public highway of the country it passes through — one might almost say, as one would say of a great river, of the country that it drains. All forms of development, including highways, drop off quickly a short distance from the right-of-way. Thus while the view from a train window is not usually a reliable indication of the country one is passing through, what is seen in this particular case is a more complete picture than the rule of thumb suggests, as would also have been true of the Canadian Pacific across the Prairies and the mountains in 1910 or so, before large-scale investment and settlement had spread over much of the territory away from the tracks. Census figures make the point neatly. As already mentioned, the 1988 Soviet census has never been released and perhaps never will be, so one must fall back on the one from 10 years earlier. It showed 21.6 million people living in Siberia, an area covering a quarter of the Asian continent. That was less than 9 per cent of the Soviet population, and most of it hugs the railway line; a few millions are found in big cities, Novosibirsk and Irkutsk, but most of the people are in thousands of desperate little settlements hacked out of the *taiga*. Along the various tracks there average about thirty inhabitants per square kilometre; in the north, the figure drops to less than one person per square kilometre. Siberia, then, has nearly as many people as Canada, but it is as though there were no Halifax, no Montreal, no Toronto, no Vancouver, only northern Quebec, northern Ontario, the Lakehead and the north generally, with perhaps two or three Winnipegs thrown in.

Siberia bears some comparison with Canada in visual terms as well. Until we neared steppe-like terrain in the last few days of the trip, as the train began its climb towards Inner Mongolia and Manchuria, the vegetation was mostly birch and fir and the topography mostly flat. After the first day or two I was reminded of the crude back-projection techniques of old Hollywood movies in which, if the scene lasted long enough and you paid close enough attention to the background, you could see the couple in the car drive past the exact same stretch of scenery time and again. Significantly, the long curve between Moscow and Japan is, and will remain for a few years yet, the last part of the world not hooked up to the fibre-optic cable system that passes around the globe like a second equator.

Nearly everyone I told about my plans for the Transsib advised me to take my own food or as much of it as I could. So when I was in London some months earlier I called on the manager of the food hamper department at Fortnum & Mason in Piccadilly and put to the test the famous claim that the shop can deliver anywhere in the world. Could they make me a custom hamper of cheeses, choice meats, marmalades, "gentlemen's relish", and so on, with a decent selection of ports and brandies, and have it waiting for me at Yaroslavl Station in Moscow at the appointed hour? The firm would be game to try on a no-fault basis, I was told, but the manager felt duty bound to inform me that he had never known one of the baskets to arrive intact anywhere inside the U.S.S.R. So I had brought my own food from Canada. I had been dragging it around with me for weeks, resisting the temptation to break into the stock during the nutritional emergencies that are so much a feature of Soviet life. I now repacked it all according to a daily menu plan and reassured myself that there was more than enough. In fact, enough to share, which is precisely what I ended up doing.

The locomotive that stood waiting for us was a Soviet-made electric engine built in 1964. The carriages were of East German construction (I suppose this is probably the last time I shall write the words *East German* except in some historical connection); they had wooden trim and were painted the standard Soviet railway green, which is brighter than dark olive but not by much. I found myself in an upper berth, sharing a compartment with a middle-aged Frenchman who came from the same gene pool as Valéry Giscard d'Estaing, and his young wife from, I gather, the French West Indies, and a heavily tattooed Siberian male of about fifty who instantly hung cheeses and sausages from the ceiling for safekeeping. In view of Gorbachev's prohibition of alcohol on the trains, he, like many of the passengers, had brought along his own supply of vodka. For the first few hours, he slept curled up around the bottles, then awoke and began swigging from one of them and discoursing loudly on the Soviet political scene. I caught the drift, which was that he saw no choice between Gorbachev and Yeltsin in that they were both scoundrels. I'm expressing the point rather more gently than I believe he was doing. As the train pitched and yawed, his cheeses and sausages swayed in unison, like the strands of a beaded curtain in some sleazy bagnio. My reading lamp was broken and the window pane was almost too caked with mud to admit light. I sensed I was in for a discouraging passage.

I was rescued by Tian Hsueh, a twenty-seven-year-old reporter from the *Commercial Times* in Taipei. We had struck up a conversation on the platform at Yaroslavl Station. His paper was sending him through Eastern Europe, the U.S.S.R., and finally China, the land his father had fled in 1948 without ever going back to. As he travelled through all the hot spots in this *annus mirabilis*, he was faxing back stories to his paper: page after page of beautiful Chinese calligraphy. Now he spotted me languishing in steerage and invited me to share his cabin, which he had all to himself. A few extra rubles made the upgrading official, and he helped me drag my luggage from one moving car to the next. A week later the reverse process would have been easier, for by then we had demolished my heavy supplies of ham, crab meat, biscuits, and gin. He was the perfect companion, full of insight and mischievous wit. We exchanged books, confidences, and professional gossip.

The country east of Moscow pretty quickly loses its urbanity, but not its history. Ancient churches, sometimes all the more imposing for the way they sit almost proudly, almost derelict, in rusty old heavy-industrial towns like Yaroslavl, can give only some hint of all the centuries of suffering that make up much of the heritage of that portion of the world: involuntary suffering and sometimes suffering deliberately sought for its spiritual benefit. Between the cities, the settlements are tiny. The wooden buildings stand in clusters — a dwelling and assorted outbuildings. Sometimes they are weatherbeaten and bare, sometimes painted a near-Wedgwood blue; in still other cases, only the traditional shutters are painted. Once we crossed the Volga River near Yaroslavl I began to sense that we were in the Russia of the Russian novels. The name Kirov alone was enough to suggest the feeling.

Kirov the city, about 950 kilometres into the journey (we reached it at 3 p.m. on the second day), was a trading centre whose history already went back 700 years when it became part of Russia in the eighteenth century and began its association with the wretched exile system. We in the West tend to think of exiles first when Siberia is mentioned and perhaps most of all political prisoners of the Stalin years. As early as 1932, five years before the infamous purges, there were 265,000 of his "special settlers" there, a figure that is more remarkable for being acknowledged than for being accurate. There is no way of knowing how many hundreds of thousands he sent to the gulags, just as there is no way of knowing how many millions he had killed in his career overall. Kirov, the person after whom the city is named, was another of those colleagues of Stalin who looked to become a rival. Stalin had him killed just as he did Trotsky. Why Kirov the city kept that name instead of reverting to its original name, Vyatka, is a mystery, considering that Perm, the next big city, a half day farther along, was allowed to drop the temporary name Molotov after Stalin's death. It's easier to change names than to restore them, I suppose.

Even in spring, life along this part of the line is hard. Vegetation alternates between birch and conifers and between both of these on the one hand and open scrub land on the other, in maddening variations and repetitions of variations. I saw one man working a wooden plough pulled by a tired shaggy horse. I couldn't learn to what extent, if any, *perestroika* had begun to penetrate here, but most of what seemed small tenancies are, I was informed, merely tiny co-ops that happen to be incredibly poor. Houses as well as gardens tend to be fenced, almost pallisaded in some cases, not merely to delineate them and keep out small pests but perhaps also to discourage larger game. The hoardings may also supplement the lines of trees used as windbreaks. It was May, but in several places there was still snow in the shadows. I got the impression that though the snow may melt, the shadows never completely disappear. There is some pasture, but it looked poor. What I noticed most were the woodpiles and how big they were in proportion to the size of the dwellings. People must spend most of the transient summer preparing as best they can for the intransigent winters.

I was making inroads on my gin supply, and so it was that I went to bed drunk in Europe and woke up hung-over in Asia. Not that I could have seen the signatory obelisk in any case, for we passed it sometime in the middle of the night, high up in the Urals. By using my pocket watch as an odometer, I calculated that we were making a top speed of over 100 kilometres per hour, but most of the time the pace was much slower and some of the time it was little short of retrograde. People were constantly getting on and getting off, so cars were being added and subtracted at some of the stations, though at other spots the train halted seemingly for no reason at all.

Sverdlovsk is a place with two claims on history: it is where Czar Nicholas and his family were murdered, back when it was called Yekaterinburg, and is close to where Francis Gary Powers, the American pilot, was shot down in his U-2 spy plane, whose existence Dwight Eisenhower flatly denied. There we had the longest scheduled stop of the whole trip — 15 minutes, to change locomotives. I have been calling the territory Siberia, but actually we were still in the Russian Federation; Siberia, strictly speaking, began only after another 250 kilometres or so, once we had reached Bogdanovich but before we got to Tyumen, a place we hit at 10 a.m., by which time I was fully awake and functioning, thanks to several glasses of strong coffee in the restaurant car that I otherwise avoided as much as possible.

The names of towns through this stretch started to take on an intoxicating ring by the simple arrangement of the syllables. Ishim, Tobolsk, Nazyvaevskaya, and finally — the name falling with the thud of end punctuation — Omsk. Most of these places were founded as long ago as the sixteenth century as forts, either for the fur traders or the Cossacks. Tobolsk was where many of the Decembrists were imprisoned after their abortive uprising in St Petersburg in 1825 (the jail has recently been given to a seminary). Omsk, whose population is now more than a million, was an *ostrog* or political prison as well; it was here that Dostoevsky served four years at hard labour. By contrast, Novosibirsk, the largest centre in Siberia, with 1.5 million people (and a subway to move them), came into existence because of the railway. This part of western Siberia is above all a land of mighty rivers — the Ob, the Tom, the Yenisei.

It was Krasnoyarsk, a large industrial city on the Yenisei, that we were heading for on the third day. By late morning, the landscape had changed; the vistas were bigger and there were rolling foothills in the distance. The human element, though as bleak as before, was changing as well. There were more abandoned buildings, though we also saw some log houses being put up, and from time to time there were small irregular pens or corrals, indicating that farming was giving way to ranching. Just when I began to get used to the wider angles, however, there would be a quick change, and the train would descend into woods once more. We passed, without stopping, many small stations, which we would not have known were stations at all but for the tattered red flags fluttering in front. Along the entire route there was a sense that the Trans-Siberian keeps shedding its skin like a snake. There are old water towers left over from the days of steam locomotives and sometimes even the steam locomotives themselves, either abandoned to the elements or relegated to shunting in the bigger marshalling yards (a distinct contrast with China, where steam is still common on the railways, thanks largely to China's abundance of coal, which is far less sulphurous than the sorts we're most familiar with in Canada). Across the whole country you see disused rolling stock by the sidings; some of it is apparently used for housing. One farmer had a root cellar made of old ties.

All of this helped to strengthen the impression that the natural world was infinitely more varied than the manmade. By the close of the day the terrain first became hillier, then took on a distinctive British Columbian case, with tall timber and big peaks. At other points the hills had sharp and unexpected twists and edges, like driftwood; the wind had put its signature on them as plainly as on, say, the Sussex Coast. By dusk we were coming up on a coal-mining town called Ilanskaya.

A policy of full disclosure compels me to admit that I was not a totally reliable witness to all of these changes. In my attempt to combat the dehydration resulting from the period of inebriation, I had broken one of my own cardinal rules of travel — always boil the drinking water for five minutes in any place, such as Siberia or Texas, where one cannot buy *The Globe and Mail*. At one stage all I could do was to place my spectacles on the night-table in such a way that I would lie in my bunk and see the Soviet Union reflected in the lenses. The impression I had then was of a horizon with serrated edges, like the metal strip used to tear lengths of Saran Wrap from the roll. Sometime during the night we passed the halfway mark between Moscow and Beijing.

Naturally enough, the closer we got to China, the more Asian faces there were on the train, and the more children as well, though some had been with us from the outset. The conductor of the Shanghai Philharmonic was aboard, for instance, along with fifteen of his musicians and all their instruments. These poor people had first gone by train from their home to Beijing, a trip of nineteen hours, there to wait in the station for the train not just to Moscow but to Leningrad, even more distant by some 1,700 kilometres or so. In that city they had played a ten-day engagement and then started back without delay. How I can't imagine, but the conductor, a round jovial man in his late forties and one of the few Chinese symphony conductors who hasn't succumbed to the brain drain, was bearing up with weary good humour. "This is the train through hell," he said, "but suffering on such a scale is food for artistic endeavour." As for my fellow westerners, they included a German middle-manager in a large computer firm, a sous-chef at the Windsor Arms Hotel in Toronto, a young English woman who wore a zircon in her left ear lobe and when I saw her was reading *Alice in Wonderland*, a couple of Kiwis with haversacks, and a cinema usher from California who kept saying *wow* and *man* and once asked Tian whether Taiwan was part of Japan. Intourist had thoughtfully sent along a guide; she had red hair (most unusual in the Soviet Union) and O-level German and a nodding acquaintance with English. That is to say, when she heard English being spoken at her, she nodded. This fostered the totally false impression that she understood at least a little bit of what was being said. She lived in Siberia, about three-quarters of the way along, and rather than teach German, as she is certified to do, she makes her living travelling back and forth, like a wooden duck in a shooting gallery.

One of the major disadvantages of life on the Transsib is that there are no facilities for bathing. This design fault becomes only too apparent after three or four days. There are small lavatories at either end of each sleeping car, but they don't have warm water. In any case, Russian signs on the doors request passengers not to attempt bathing. I gather that the tone is rather more abrupt than that of the famous signs once found in the men's loo of the British Museum Reading Room, put there to keep Karl Marx and his disreputable friends from continuing to treat the place like a hotel: "These basins are for casual ablutions only". I tried breaking the rule, first filling a goatskin bag with hot water from the *batchok*, the boiler from which people make tea and on which the resident guard-chambermaid in each carriage cooks her rude meals. But I had no sooner mixed the scalding water with the cold when the martinet in question, having seen me siphon off the water, came pounding on the locked WC door, demanding an explanation and threatening punishment. After that I was careful to take only enough water to fill a metal cup I carried, as though I were indeed brewing tea. I found that by diluting it and not wasting a drop, I could wash my hair — sort of — or bathe — again, after a fashion — on alternating days; but the level of hygiene never really exceeded what one might expect in, say, a jail house in Karachi. Yet I was luckier than the people who were also dependent on the system for all their meals. The food started out quite adequate by Soviet standards. Terrible meats and not many vegetables but lots of subsidized bread (the fresh loaves were stored under the seats in the booths the diners sat in) and a few local delicacies, such as yoghurt taken aboard in the kind of glass milk bottles that even the English haven't seen for years. But the quality deteriorated quickly, I observed, and with it the quantity. The last meal before the Chinese border was a piece of volcanic cheese and two bits of salami, all of which people soon had to forfeit to the Chinese health authorities who searched the cars for animal and vegetable products that might be diseased. At times I felt quite guilty, eating strawberries and turkey and granola, though the guilt passed more quickly than the landscape.

Some of the places remain in my memory almost by accident. Tayshet, 4,522 kilometres east of Moscow, is distinguished only by being sited where the mainline meets the line running north to the mammoth hydro dam at Bratsk, which I recalled because of Yevtushenko's long poem "Bratsk Station". I remember grassy hillsides, too, and the smiling, worn-out faces of local people for whom the arrival of the train, even though it did not stop, might, to the extent that it relieves the tedium, be one of the high points of their day. There was also one spectacular cemetery, spread over the slope of a hillside but confined within a fence, as most everything manmade in those parts is; some of the markers were at precarious angles but they were freshly painted and had been carved in the same manner as the door- and window-frames of the local houses. The graves of exiles, I thought, political or otherwise. As I believe Farley Mowat has noted, Siberia seems to serve the same social function that the Yukon sometimes does in Canada: young people go there to break away and older people to start over.

The last considerable city on the Soviet side of the route is Irkutsk, where we rolled, slammed, and hissed to a stop at 9:30 a.m. on the fourth day. It is famous for having once been called the Paris of Siberia. That seems a reckless use of hyperbole, though the place does have an interesting history. Some of the Decembrists were sent there, and later a gold rush of sorts took place near by.

The main attraction of this part of Siberia is Lake Baikal, which the rail line follows for nearly half its total circumference after first hugging one of the main rivers feeding it. Because it is the world's deepest lake (1,741 metres; Lake Ontario by comparison reaches a depth of only 237 metres), Baikal is said to contain 20 per cent of the world's fresh water reserves, and it is the habitat of many creatures and plants not found elsewhere. Siberians are said to refer to it sometimes as the Siberian Sea, and it does seem a tiny ecological world of its own, occupying the space between ranges of mountains, tipped by birch forests and, when we passed by in early May, still thick with ice pile-ups quite far from shore.

Even the most recent editions of some of the best-known English-language guidebooks rave on about the purity of the water and the generally paradisiacal nature of the whole environment there. The Soviets know better. Pulp and paper mills have been dumping waste into the lake for many years, and cities like Irkutsk have contributed their sewage; the writer Valentin Rasputin became an important public figure as much as a literary one after his advocacy of Baikal's cause, in somewhat the same manner as Igor Shkliarevsky, more recently, with respect to Chernobyl. The government has done a great deal in response to the situation, not only in banning log rafts but also in building a pipeline to take Irkutsk's waste far away. Moscow claims that the water is now 50 per cent cleaner than it was a few years ago, yet species continue to die, and even the authorities have estimated that 20 billion rubles would have to be spent on a proper clean-up. One of the effects of the emerging economic order in Eastern Europe and South Asia is that Moscow, and the world, have begun to recognize that the damage done to the environment and health under a rigid planned economy is no less than under open-throttle capitalism. Poland, for example, is easily the most polluted nation on the whole European continent. Siberia is said to be the second-largest source of oxygen on Earth, after the now quickly disappearing rainforests of the Amazon basin. Acknowledging the fact may not be Gorbachev's first priority, but he seems much more aware of such matters than his predecessors or even most of his neighbours.

We hit Ulan Ude the next night. This was once a very important stop for caravans going to China — our first clue that we were within hope of getting to the People's Republic, still a thousand kilometres away at the nearest point. It is also here that the line veers off to Beijing, the easy way, through Mongolia. By late the next morning we were stopped at Karymskaya, near where we took the track to Manchuria instead. The countryside to the north and south, but especially to the south, resembled steppes, and there were mounted shepherds with Mongolian features tending their sheep and goats from the saddle. There was also trash strewn all along the roadbed by generations of train crews. In only thirty-six hours or so we would be in Beijing, though eight or more would be spent straddling the border.

In China and virtually all other major countries, the distance between the rails is 141.25 centimetres, but the Soviets use a different gauge — 150 centimetres. People commonly suppose that this indicates Russian backwardness. On the contrary, the Soviets have adhered to the safer, more expensive standard while the other countries, one by one, have sacrificed stability to savings, though there are other factors involved as well. By clinging to the older size, the Soviets have heightened security at the frontier and generally reduced the risk of invasion by rail. So it is that at Zabaikalsk, the last point in the U.S.S.R., 6,293 kilometres from Moscow, we turned in our visas and filed into a huge old building with Corinthian pillars to exchange our leftover rubles for dollars. Meanwhile, the train was taken away so that the bogies on all the cars could be changed. Lingering in the smelly, overcrowded station, it was easy to chafe at the waste of time, but the wait was as nothing compared with the ten hours one might expect on a train crossing from India to Pakistan or vice versa, for delays of that magnitude result mainly when the two nations despise each other, and it was clear despite the presence of some soldiers with rifles that tensions were much relaxed here. Foreigners were even allowed to take photographs of the platform, an activity forbidden at many another, less sensitive facility of the Soviet Railways.

Finally we reboarded and progressed 12 kilometres until Manzhouli, where Chinese immigration officials climbed aboard and there was a wait of several hours more, during which a Chinese dining car full of delicious food took the place of the long-empty Russian one. A patriotic Chinese locomotive — Chinese locomotives have names like East Wind, Red in the East, or Progress — was added as well. At the station where we changed our freshly retrieved dollars for Chinese Foreign Exchange Certificates, the yuan used by foreigners, was a large notice-board hung with news photographs; I was told that sometimes the display shows the likenesses of recently executed criminals. Nevertheless, I couldn't help but breathe easier now that I was in China, notwithstanding the present perception that it and not the U.S.S.R. is the more obstinate and authoritarian place. The officials were courteous as well as efficient. A customs inspector, age twenty-three, came into our compartment and asked if he might sit down and join me in a conversation to practise his English. To my disappointment, he mentioned Dr Norman Bethune, whose name I had hoped to travel in China without either hearing or speaking, just as I was resolved not to give people any bloody Maple Leaf pins for their lapels. Alas, there was even a toast to the old boy at a banquet in Chongqing thrown by the local newspaper editors.

Anyway, the train got up steam, and we set off to see a bit of Inner Mongolia and then Manchuria. I looked out the window to find two Chinese soldiers looking in. One had his rifle slung upside down; the other was unarmed and the sleeves of his tunic were far too long for his arms; they smiled. Tian and I got into the gin once more to celebrate.

We awoke the next morning, our sixth on the train, just in time to catch a glimpse of Angangxi, whose notoriety is its proximity to Tsitsihar (now Qigihar), where there is a public space once devoted to the execution of bandits and other wrongdoers. The belief in those days was that people who died with parts of their bodies missing could not be admitted to Heaven, and the prisoners, once decapitated, had their heads sewn back on — but backwards, so they wouldn't be mistaken for the righteous. At breakfast we were at Daqing, a city synonymous with oil wells; we saw numerous small ones pumping away in the middle of the fields, and a refinery and a pipeline in the distance. By lunch we were in Harbin, just beyond the banks of the Pine Flower River. This was once a White Russian stronghold, a fact that recalls one of the most colourful incidents in the history of the whole Trans-Siberian system. When the Bolsheviks pulled out of the First World War, the Czech Legion was left stranded, with the Bolsheviks now hostile to them, certain that they would join up with the White forces. With their way back to Europe blocked and nothing to lose, the Czechs hijacked the trains and shot their way across Siberia towards Vladivostok. By teatime we had crossed into Jilin Province and were at Changchun, its capital. It was once the centre of the puppet state established by the Japanese, with Pu-Yi, the last emperor of China, as its titular head.

The deeper we penetrated into China, the more complex, and inexpressible, became Tian's feelings about his ancestral home, which he had visited only once before, a year earlier, right after the Tiananmen massacre. The event had affected him very deeply, more deeply than I could imagine or he could articulate. Around Changchun we passed, again without stopping or even tooting the throaty whistle, a series of small stations, each bearing a family name as the name of the community or district.

"My father tells me that when he was a boy, about 90 per cent of the people in the county of the province where he lived had the same family name", Tian said. "In China there is only the self and the concept of the family. There is no Chinese ideogram to express the idea of personal privacy, for instance. And because there is no personal privacy there is no corresponding sense of what is public responsibility. Until that breaks down it will be a stumbling block to democracy. They don't know that democracy is not something you do for yourself or your family. It's supposed to be for the public good. All that will take time."

He was looking out the window. He appeared wistful but determined. When I looked out the same window I couldn't help but see how much less harsh life here seemed to be than it did in the U.S.S.R.

Northeast China is one of the most thickly industrialized regions, yet like the rest of the country it is under intense cultivation, with hardly the smallest bit of arable land left untilled. Its people are supposed to be strong, silent, and self-reliant: it's a Chinese cliché. Everybody was working hard. They worked in the factories, which are decorated with slogans such as "We must be happy to work here so that we will be happy to return home" or "We must keep this plant safe so that we can produce goods for the safety of society". Or they work in the fields or paddies. But everyone is busy and everyone is in motion constantly, without the almost paralytic despair I sensed so often across the Soviet Union.

In Siberia I saw surprisingly few farm animals, and many of those I did were so emaciated I could count their ribs. I remember one poor cow that was covered in sores as well.

China was full of healthy animals — ducks, goats, sheep, everything, all making noise at once; even lots of dogs, which I hadn't expected. At one point, the tracks were clogged with cows, a scene reminiscent of India except that these were fat, happy cows and their presence, I believe, the result of a bovine jailbreak. Farm machinery was abundant too. Much of it was recent, though the new stuff coexisted with the simplest type of plough. Such juxtaposition was typical. Later in my stay I saw people working on the long-term project of building a reservoir. First bulldozers had cleared the way; now hundreds of men worked with spades and wheelbarrows and wicker baskets to complete the job. A westerner would say, Why not use heavy equipment and complete the whole project in a short time with only a handful of personnel? The Chinese would answer: And what will all the remaining people do the rest of the year? Westerner: Why, they'd make more bulldozers in a bulldozer factory, of course. . . . The idea seems incomprehensible to the Chinese, who fear that the present system, one of the greatest organizational feats in human history perhaps and certainly an extraordinary improvement over generations of bloody tyranny by a patchwork quilt of Nationalists, bandits, and warlords, might begin to unravel. Hence the tightened grip on political power even while economic power is being freed up ever so slowly. This lies at the heart of the contrast with the Soviet Union. Gorbachev could change all at once, as Poland did, with chaotic results, or change slowly, with a combination of both political and economic reforms, hoping that the speed will prove neither too fast nor too slow and the mixture not too volatile. At what point does decay make change inevitable? At what point is change decay and not progress?

Last year an auto factory in this northeastern part of China manufactured 80,000 lorries, though the government had placed orders for only 60,000 or so. Without recourse to layoffs or even variable production schedules, the plant continues to churn them out to keep everyone working, filling up huge carparks with light trucks. Meanwhile, in southern and western China, production of staple commodities lags far behind. The small enterprise businesses, which were the first hint of reform when they began springing up throughout China in numbers almost beyond counting, seemed to offer the best hope of acting as a pressure gauge for use in making the difficult adjustment; at the least they were an acknowledgement of the marketplace as a legitimate consideration within the total economic equation. That the Chinese are such irrepressible entrepreneurs, whether in the state's service or their own, is after all one of the reasons they are able to feed themselves, a quarter of the world's population. But since September 1988, the government's strict credit policy, introduced to fight inflation, has forced more than 3 million small businesses to close. God only knows what the effects of the political crackdown have been.

I looked out the window just as a young pig took it into its head to chase the train, as a puppy might chase a car. It ran after us for several carriage-lengths, its big ears flopping in the wind. People were building houses and then building courtyard walls around them, often with shards of glass set along the top to discourage thieves but also perhaps to reinforce the idea of the family compound — and of family solidarity against outside forces. People were buying and others were selling. Women were carrying strange vegetables and men were carrying tools. Motorbikes became conspicuous among the bicycles. Most older people still wore shapeless blue Mao suits, but the young affected the western look, especially in their footwear, which you could tell they were proud of by the way they walked. Everyone seemed to be rushing somewhere under the weight of a great unseen burden, physical or psychological. Kids in a schoolyard played basketball with grown-up intensity, for they were doing more than passing time or taking exercise. We had journeyed into the middle of some spectacle that the participants for some reason didn't seem to recognize as such. Eventually, when the light had failed completely, I went to bed, though reluctantly. I woke up the next morning in time to pack and re-sort and clean myself up and dispose of the rubbish before we came to a stop at Beijing at 6:35 a.m. We had been on the train for one week and had come exactly 9,001 kilometres. Nine thousand and two would have been too many.

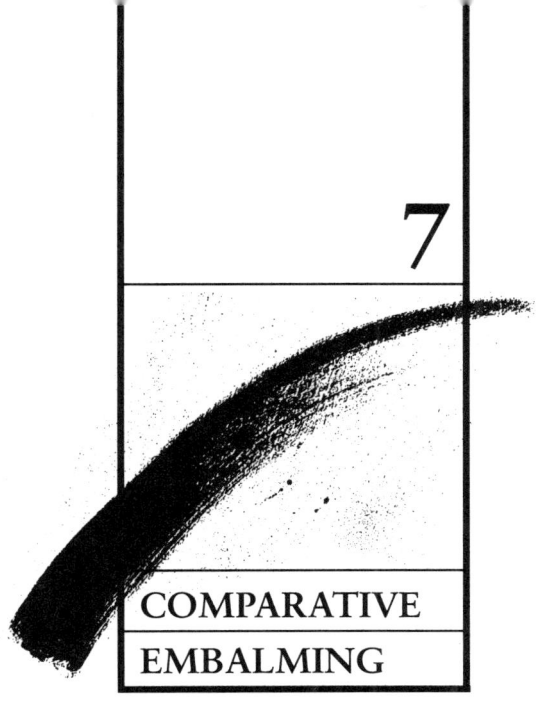

7
COMPARATIVE EMBALMING

In a few days' time it would be the first anniversary of the student hunger strike that led, a couple of weeks later, to the tragedy in Tiananmen Square. Accordingly, Beijing was on edge. It would not be overstating the case to say that the joint was crawling with cops. And soldiers. And even, for some reason, sailors, their shiny helmets incongruous with their traditional blouses and scarves. "Those people on the street corners who look like secret police", a western diplomat explained to me. "They're secret police." The day I arrived the government announced that it was freeing 211 of the dissidents who had been taken alive, including one major figure; 431 others were still being "investigated"; this was the second such release since the incident. It was thought to be designed to curb the threat that the U.S. Congress might try to take away

China's most-favoured-nation status, but of course the principal reason was to avoid or lessen dissent on the June fourth anniversary. Feelings were running high on both sides, and it was easy to make matters worse. While I was there I saw a telecast of the Cable News Network from Atlanta reporting a speech in Beijing by the CNN's founder, Ted Turner. He had the temerity to tell the audience that he felt sympathy for the soldiers who had done the shooting. He later backtracked by way of apology.

All this tension was brought home to me the moment I stepped off the train. Someone was calling my name, though I hadn't expected to be met. The person introduced himself as Wen Dong of the All-China Journalists' Association. I had got by in the U.S.S.R. without a handler and I thought that I would avoid one here as well. But I was quickly faced with an ultimatum. I could cancel all my existing tickets and accommodations (they were prepaid, alas) and buy completely new ones both for myself and Wen, who would accompany me everywhere. Or I could go to the foreign affairs ministry to plead for an exemption from the tough new restrictions on foreign journalists (which no one had yet been exempted from). The cost of the Chinese portion of my trip had just been trebled and the amount of slack reduced to — well, I didn't know to what level.

Despite various enquiries in Moscow with many relevant individuals, I never did succeed in learning why the exchange with *Oktyabr* had fallen through, except that it had something to do with the uneasy nature of the co-operation between Novosti and the Soviet foreign service. People and agencies blamed one another, Ottawa saying it was Moscow's decision and Moscow insisting it was Ottawa's. In Beijing, matters were more straightforward. "To be blunt about it," I was told bluntly when the time finally came for me to hint safely at the question, "we didn't want you here. Your visa request was first turned down and then you got your foreign minister to intercede. The situation is uncertain, and more foreign journalists aren't welcome in the present atmosphere. We've been widely criticized for this decision but it's a matter of safety." Later titbits convinced me of what I had suspected all along, that my original request to the association had not been lost at all but simply ignored in the hope that I would go away, for in my desire to get a head start on the paperwork, I had inadvertently made myself the first North American since the massacre to ask for a visiting journalist's permit for the capital. In any case, there I was in the company of Wen Dong, thirty-five, a fellow of quick humour and a skilled expeditor. He had many contacts in the West. His wife, the daughter of the Chinese ambassador to Egypt, is a student in Toronto, and Wen himself is widely travelled; he had recently been to England, for example, as the guest of Sir David English of the *Daily Mail*. A good companion, it seemed to me, so I resolved to make the best of the situation and to see and learn what I could.

Several months earlier, Taiwan had decided to permit its citizens free egress to visit the People's Republic for pleasure or business, even though, despite the increasingly important economic ties binding them together, the two countries remain officially at war. The idea was that the Taiwanese would see socialism at first hand and soon return home thankful for the Kuomintang (which while I was crossing Siberia made a move even further to the right, installing a former general, Hau Pei-tsun, as premier). The practical effect of this liberalization in the midst of capitalist authoritarianism was that China was suddenly full of tourists from Taiwan. They were all the more conspicuous because there were so few from the West with whom to contrast them.

At the luxury-class joint-venture hotel to which I hurried, ravenous for a hot shower and some news in English, the ratio of staff to guest rooms would normally, I should think, be about two-to-one, as it would be in an equivalent hotel in Europe or North America. Such had been the drop in tourism following Tiananmen Square that I shouldn't be surprised if the figure was ten-to-one. I saw not even a handful of westerners there and not many more in Beijing as a whole. But then people were keeping out of sight. It didn't seem to me that the danger of another uprising was very great. Such, at least, was what instinct and common sense told me; there might be a commemorative disturbance, perhaps, but the leading democrats were in prison, in exile, or dead. It was simply a case of rumour and anxiety feeding on themselves, but there was enough danger of another kind, I suppose. Wiser heads than mine were keeping low.

The journalists' association made it plain that they didn't wish me hanging around Beijing for long, yet I managed to enjoy it for several days at least. I believe it is a city that Canadians usually take to. The main streets are tree-lined and spacious, and the pace is slow compared with that of most other capitals its size, even Moscow. I feel that the climate favours it, too, though many would disagree. In summer, it is hot and dry, with a wind blowing in from the Gobi. As recently as the 1940s, water was hauled in by camel; there was little dust when I was there, though two weeks earlier the city had suffered its fourth dust storm of the year. In winter, it's beastly cold, but there is seldom enough snow to impede bicycles. These are the main means of transport despite an adequate bus system and a modern subway (for the construction of which, in the 1960s, Mao ordered the razing of the 500-year-old city walls, one of the larger acts of wanton destruction to take place during the Cultural Revolution). My secret theory is that people prefer bicycles as tiny acts of rebellion against the system and against their own Confucian deference to authority, in somewhat the same way that most Soviets simply lay their seat-belts loosely across their laps without buckling them, adhering to the spirit of the law while violating the letter of it. To ride the bus or subway is to cast your destiny with that of strangers, far beyond family. To ride a bike (one costs an average office worker perhaps two months' salary) is to stay in control. In any case, the scarcity of automobiles, like the abundance of horse-drawn wagons and pedicab drivers, adds to the comparatively low levels of pollution and high level of history. The second of these is sometimes an illusion, however.

If there were still an emperor to look down from the higher structures in the Forbidden City, he would see a number of construction cranes and massive electronic advertisements. The change in name from Peking to Beijing has a symbolic importance reflecting more than just the administrative shift to *pinyin*, for, since 1949, in fact since the early 1960s, the city has been virtually replaced by another one built on the same spot. Some historical buildings remain, but then the Chinese way is to rebuild historical monuments exactly as they were before, so that continuity is more important than the true age of anything. The most famous section of the Great Wall open to visitors, at Badaling, about 70 kilometres northwest of the city, dates from both the second century B.C., when it was built as a communication line across the top of razorback mountains almost impregnable against either mounted or dismounted enemy, and equally from 1957, when it was rebuilt with the same materials. The second time, handrails were included; they're necessary; the thin line of tourists climbing up to the top, almost hand-over-hand to an elevation of a thousand metres, resembles nothing so much as cheechakos going over the Chilkoot Pass in 1898. Or take the Temple of Heaven, built in 1420 and again in 1890 and then restored in the 1970s. In China, history is everywhere and yet it's never quite tangible the way it often is in the West; westerners in China find it hard to experience the sensation of the distant past being right at their elbow, even when at the site of great events, even in the Forbidden City, amazing though it is in its complexity and scope. History, in China, is more a question of landscape and of streetscape than of individual buildings and monuments. The Ming Tombs seem less "historical" than the mountains surrounding them, which appear to have been painted with a calligrapher's brush.

All of which is to say that Beijing seems very crisp, very modern, very clean. The big western hotels and other such joint ventures work in a way that their Soviet equivalents do not. It is not a case of Beijing being a tourist trap exactly. I was actually slightly shocked to drive past Tiananmen Square and see the Great Hall of the People and the huge portrait of Mao atop the Gate of Heavenly Peace. Such places look like postcards of themselves. One looks with morbid curiosity at the spot where the students erected the so-called Goddess of Democracy statue. (However much I sympathize with the cause, however much I see the site becoming a sort of shrine in the history of anti-authoritarianism, like the Decembrists' square or the Eureka Stockade only more vast in its significance, I remember thinking what bad taste it was to imitate the Americans' Statue of Liberty — the poor people were so cut off that they bought the premise of America being synonymous with freedom or of having an exclusive claim to the democratic tradition.)

This is a long-winded way of saying that Beijing does not especially seem like a city for foreigners. It is more or less up to date without the least pretence of being fashionable, and even after all these years it must be a hardship posting for diplomats and executives, at least emotionally. But neither does it seethe with its own importance, as Washington does or once did, or as I have no doubt Tokyo does. For all their power, the eunuchs in the Forbidden City trod softly, and their successors still adhere to this approach. What sticks out most forcefully about Beijing is that it is probably a delightful place for the elderly. I saw them everywhere. Old women whose feet were once bound — they still exist. Old men with white beards who play chess and listen to Beijing opera in the park surrounding the Temple of Heaven. They patronize the Bird Market, where parakeets are sold by the thousands along with parrots, goldfish, lizards, turtles, monkeys — all manner of small creatures, even worms. (Walking through, I could imagine how the activity there might be reported by the western media: "Goldfish were active today amid renewed inflation fears while worms were sluggish and turtles moved slowly. . . .") In these days when taxi drivers make a thousand yuan in a month and an independent businessman as much as 10,000 during the same period, one wonders what will happen to the elderly, one of the city's great resources, the only one perhaps that hasn't been reconstructed in the recent past.

Only one public statue of Mao remains in the capital, though it is colossal. Like Lenin's, his memory has been undergoing downward revision. In Mao's case, the process began with his death in 1976 and has not been without sharp upturns along the way. One facile illustration of the difference between Mao's stature and Lenin's is that the queues are much, much shorter at the former's mausoleum than at the latter's — only about ten or fifteen minutes' wait.

While I stood in line to pursue my newfound interest in comparative embalming (I was looking forward to gazing on the body of Ho Chi Minh in a couple of weeks' time), a professor of Japanese, who had been removed to manual labour in the countryside during the Cultural Revolution, gave me the current line on Mao. "His theme was constant struggle rather than gradual change. He was a very great man of course, but he was narrow in his outlook. Except for the Soviet Union he never set foot in any other country than China." Such language teachers are in a particularly vulnerable position. The western view is that the democracy movement was born and peopled by students at Beijing University on the city's northwest side. In China much of the suspicion is focused more narrowly, on the adjacent campus of the much smaller Qinghua University, which houses the foreign languages institute and is always littered with Americans and other bad influences.

Mao's ghost is at the centre of a paradox. His policies are held to blame for much that is wrong with the present but are also reverted to for safety when the present brings uncertainty. He opposed all forms of population control, for example, believing that China was a peasant that needed as large a family as possible to work the land. Now, when the resources are stretched even more dangerously beyond capacity, he is rebuked, but the remedy is sought in a typically Maoist scheme — punishing women who have a second child, usually by taking away their jobs, even though both parents' incomes are necessary to feed the permissible family of three. Since Tiananmen Square, Maoism, as a thing in itself distinct from both socialism and Mao the man, has been creeping back. One day a person called my attention to some music coming out over a public address system. "These are political songs of the early 1960s, songs about struggle. They were played all the time just before the Cultural Revolution. It was recently decreed that they be revived."

I had absolutely no reason whatever to believe that the authorities were keeping an eye on me except through the gentle agency of the All-China Journalists' Association, but I shouldn't have been surprised to learn that they were. (I had no equivalent suspicion while in the Soviet Union.)

Moscow: The Kalinin Prospeckt, a Western-style shopping street for which long rows of historical Russian houses were pulled down.

Harry Vinogradov, the unofficial artist known as Bicapo, in his Moscow studio.

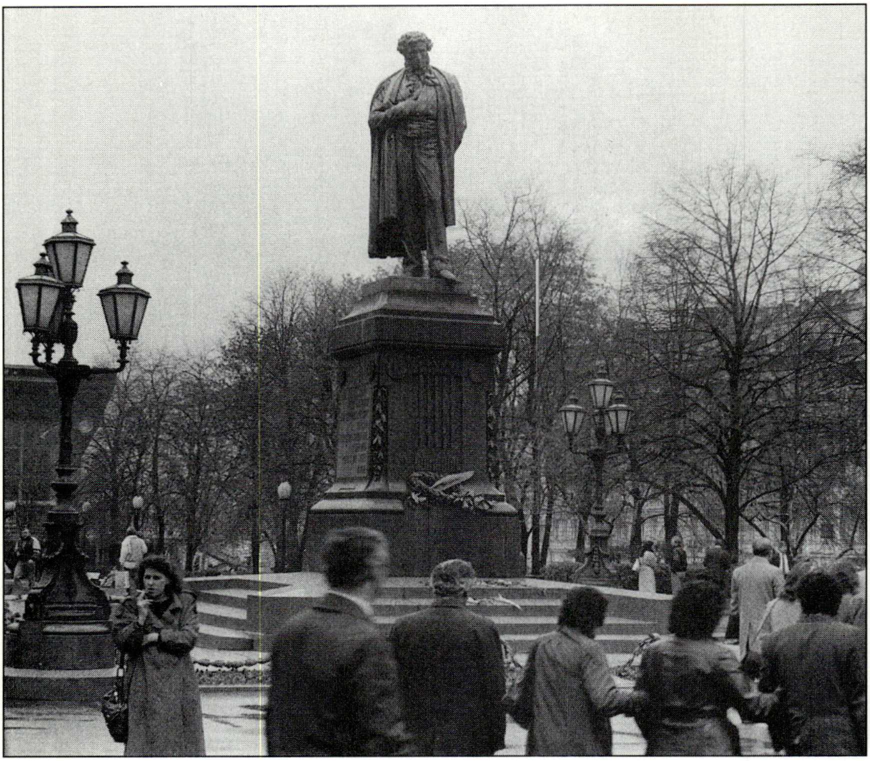

ИЗВЕСТИЯ СОВЕТОВ НАРОДНЫХ ДЕПУТАТОВ СССР

Газета выходит с марта 1917 года • № 246 (23149) • Московский выпуск • Воскресенье, 2 сентября 1990 года • Цена 3 коп.

События, факты, мнения

НА ПУТИ К ОПТИМАЛЬНЫМ РЕШЕНИЯМ

Президент СССР отвечает на вопросы журналистов

ЗАСЕДАНИЕ СОВЕТА ОБОРОНЫ

О встрече М. С. Горбачева с Дж. Бушем

ПРЯМАЯ СВЯЗЬ

ГОРОДСКОЙ СОВЕТ ПРИГЛАШАЕТ МИНИСТРА

Подписка началась

ИТОГИ СОВМЕСТНОГО ЗАСЕДАНИЯ СОВЕТА ФЕДЕРАЦИИ И ПРЕЗИДЕНТСКОГО СОВЕТА СССР

РЕШЕНИЕ АННУЛИРОВАНО

НОВЫЕ РУКОВОДИТЕЛИ КГБ и МВД

Создана группа дружбы

За открытие границы

Забастовка в Западном Бейруте

Амнистия

Встретимся колокольным звоном

Будет ли памятник Сальвадору Альенде?

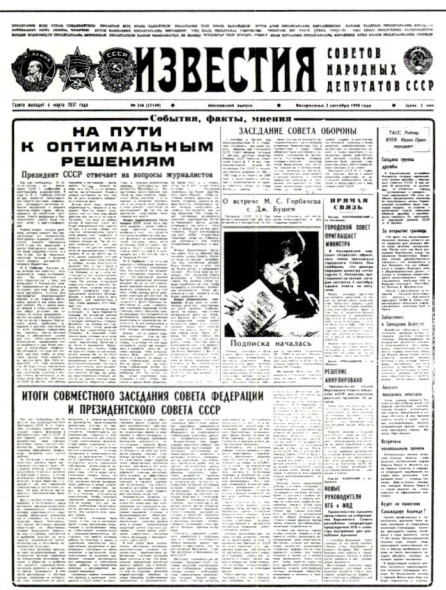

Pushkin Square in Moscow, where a perplexing variety of newspapers are bought, read and argued over.

Izvestia—*like* Pravda, *a victim of shifting political allegiances. Its readership dwindles while liberal journals rise to new circulation levels: in the case of* Arguments and Facts, *34 million copies.*

A Moscow art cinema.

Leningrad: The columns of St Isaac's Cathedral still bear some scars from the Great Patriotic War.

May Day: Towards the Historical Museum I could see columns mustering, banners, brightly coloured groups of walkers pacing like horses in the paddock, impatient for the race to begin.

The People's Liberation Army, like the Public Security Bureau, was in evidence everywhere.

A Beijing street musician.

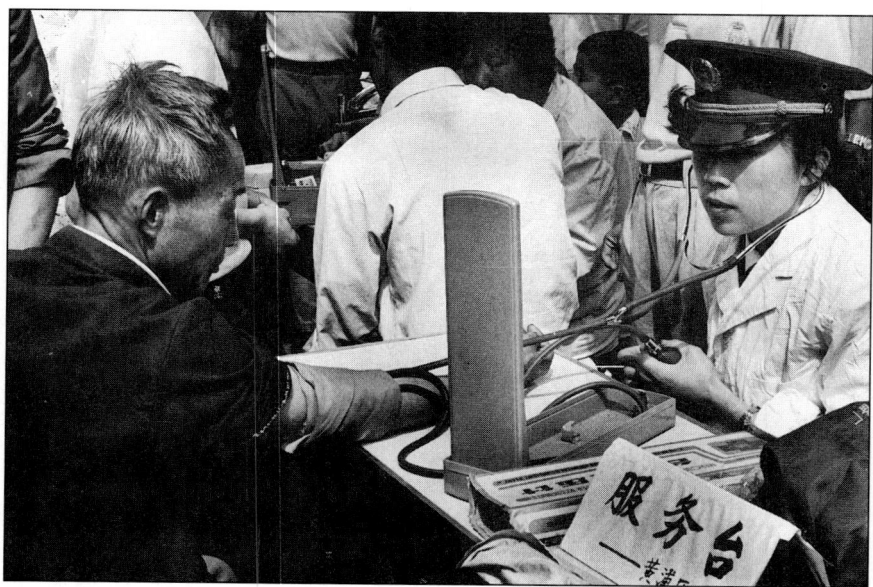

In the aftermath of the Tiananmen Square massacre, the People's Liberation Army was assigned various public-relations tasks, such as administering free blood-pressure tests in Shanghai.

The thin line of tourists climbing to the top of the Great Wall, almost hand over hand to an elevation of 1,000 metres, resembles nothing so much as cheechakos crossing the Chilkoot Pass in 1898.

Chongqing is cut into the side of a mountain that sits at the place where the Jialing River, strong, wide and imposing, gives up its identity and joins the Yangtze.

A shooting gallery at East Lake park in Wuhan.

A market vendor in Thousand Families Street in Wuhan.

Chongqing still retains much of its traditional Chinese buildings.

A market in one of Shanghai's former foreign concessions (note the European windows).

A Hong Kong slum.

Hong Kong's three classes: the sampan, the Star ferry and the QE2.

A sign of the future: The most conspicuous new building in Hong Kong, and perhaps its most obvious manmade landmark, is the tower of the state bank of the PRC, the Bank of China.

Given even the possibility that I might have been followed, I therefore took a foolish risk in making a rendezvous with Tian from the train, for I might have brought him to official notice as well. I told him as much when we met for dinner. I offered the opinion that he was putting too much faith in his appearance and his fluent Mandarin to carry him along unnoticed, especially in that he carried a visitor's permit describing himself as a "merchant" but had papers showing clearly that he was nothing of the sort, but an undercover journalist intending to report on the June fourth anniversary. We discussed all this at a Muslim restaurant called Coming Smoothly from the East, a steamy unpainted room above some small shops. When we left, we hired a pedicab. As we got underway, the elderly hunchbacked driver asked Tian whether I was a Pakistani — he knew there was some sort of Pakistani delegation in town and I was so white that he thought I might be part of it. I was glad that we clopped along through narrow alleys near Long North Street because it showed there was absolutely no one behind us as far as the eye could see. We wound our way through the maze to emerge in traffic once again, engendering one or two near-accidents in the process.

At one point we turned a corner and came face to face with an enormous billboard with emphatic red type two metres high on a white background. It dwarfed the nearby buildings and looked so exclamatory that I thought it must certainly contain some reference to foreign devils. Tian laughed. "It says, 'Drive your bicycle on the right-hand side.'" Some do and some don't. "It promises unspecified punishments for those who disobey. This is typical in that the threat is general and also large — far out of proportion to the violation." Thus alerted, I spotted a number of English signs in China that bear him out. This one, for example — "There is a fine for both offences! Please do not spit and littering!" — with the penalty before the misdemeanours. Tian professed to find significance in this, as it fit his theory about the Chinese family as a concept and as a stumbling block to further social progress by way of some form of democratic movement. In former times, the Chinese man, once married, would begin to ready himself for his death, the second great event in the existence of the family. Whether a northerner or southerner, he would prepare his own coffin, giving it pride of place in the courtyard of the home and finishing it with expensive lacquers, one coat per year; visitors might tell the age of a very old man by the thickness and brilliance of the finish, as one might count the rings of a tree. Tian's point was that some of the underlying assumptions remain. "The Chinese people are difficult to motivate because of the family", he told me — the long history of the peasant rebellions, large and small, notwithstanding. Beijing is unopposed as the site of the Olympics for the year 2000. When I was there, preparations were underway for the Asia Games to be held in four months' time, which would serve as a small-scale dress rehearsal. It was to accommodate the expected crowds that the authorities had recently rewritten some of the local traffic regulations, changing the direction of certain one-way streets and the like. Some people professed that this was merely part of a more subtle plan to preclude any crowds of protesters from assembling in the centre of the city.

As Tian and I rode along we passed Tiananmen Square. Normally at that time, after offices, factories, and schools let out, it would be full of strollers and lollers, and on Sundays it would be especially crowded, with children flying huge dragon-kites. Locals have been banned on Sundays now, and Chinese from other cities are scarcer than before, just as the number of foreigners is way down. The Sunday I was in attendance only one kite was evident. It was small and simple and was being flown by an old man from the countryside. He had apparently been hired for that purpose. Without expression, he stood tending the end of the long cord, watched by dozens of troops with automatic weapons.

8

CHONGQING!

A ir travel within China is not highly developed. To the extent that this means that it is also not terribly efficient, the result can be frustrating. Flying us out of Beijing, Wen Dong confirmed that our plane was to leave at 6 p.m., as the printed schedule stated. We arrived at the airport at 4:30 to learn that the departure had been put back to 3:20. Fortunately, the flight was delayed and wouldn't be taking off until seven. We went to the proper gate, where the NOW BOARDING sign was flashing even though the aircraft had not yet arrived. When it did appear, we nearly missed it because the gate was changed at the last minute and no one told us. Such difficulties are more than made up for by the fact that rail, land, and river travel are cheap and convenient. By flying to Chongqing, a place I had always wanted to visit, we were going to put this to the test.

Chinese airports tend to be small and simple. Beijing's is what you would expect in the West for a provincial city with only 5 per cent of Beijing's population. Chongqing's, stuck up in the mountains of Sichuan, 2,500 kilometres to the southwest, was even more basic.

We were met at our destination by a woman of about 25 who was to be our driver. She first corrected her posture behind the wheel and tested the pedals. Then she neatly folded the hem of her skirt back to the knees, exposing the tops of her stockings, and put on a pair of white gloves of thin cotton, the kind that archivists wear when handling rare maps. Whereupon she took off like a drag racer, sometimes veering into the parallel lane and honking the horn at every opportunity, however remote the danger. We threaded our way down through the mountains, which are planted in corn or winter wheat above, overlooking rice paddies in the valleys below. Given the repressed or at least rigidly private nature of sexuality in contemporary China, I was somewhat surprised when we passed a topless woman standing all alone in the middle of the road, staring into space. "There are many mental patients in this area", I was informed. "Their families cannot always afford to send them for treatment in some other city and so they are given work on farms here." As we pulled up to the hotel, three prostitutes were standing out front, spitting on the steps. They were only part-time prostitutes. During the day they worked hard as illegal money-changers.

Growing up in the 1950s and '60s, just on the cusp of the Cultural Revolution, I read many books on China in which Chongqing, under its former name Chung King, played an important role. The foreign correspondents of the Second World War, such as Edgar Snow and Theodore H. White, wrote of it when it was both the capital of China and what one writer called "the most heavily bombed city in history" (this was before the Blitz, before Dresden, and of course before Hiroshima). The humanists, such as Robert Payne and Lin Yutang, wrote of it in much the same terms: as a remote, backward place that had suddenly been thrust into the spotlight of world history and subjected to the horror of modern warfare.

Chongqing is cut into the side of a mountain that sits at the place where the Jialing River, strong, wide, and imposing, gives up its identity and joins the Yangtze. Thus in its situation it bears some superficial resemblance to Pittsburgh; but it is a primal Pittsburgh on a grand and profane scale. At the point where the rivers meet there is a long series of steep stone steps carved out of the mountainside. For centuries, hundreds, maybe thousands of water-coolies trudged up and then down, in a constant single motion, bringing the city's drinking water directly from the Jialing, where dead bodies and who knows what else floated by. In about 1920, the English adventurer One-Arm Sutton conceived of a plan to build a modern waterworks in Chongqing. He had come to China to help the warlords after a career mining gold in Siberia. But he wasn't able to put down a revolt by the coolies, who were fearful that they would lose their livelihood such as it was, and not until the 1950s, after the communists took over, was the old system replaced. Chongqing is full of stories like that. I found the place wonderful, even in some ways I hadn't quite expected.

It was one of the last of the treaty ports, opened to European and American power only as late as 1890, but there are no foreign concessions there as rude reminders of the days of swagger and extraterritoriality. There never were many western traders there, only western scoundrels like Sutton or his contemporary Two-Gun Cohen, the Canadian who became probably the world's most successful spy, greater than Dusko Popov, the Yugoslav who inspired James Bond, greater even than Sidney Reilly, who nearly succeeded in ending the Russian Revolution almost before it

could begin. Today there aren't many westerners of any kind in Chongqing. Air travel being as already described, the city is still reached most commonly by boat. Recently China has established a state-run adventure-tour company to lure American rafters to the white-water areas nearer the source of the Yangtze, but Chongqing, in the middle stretches of that enormously long river, is as free from foreigners as Shanghai, an equal distance in the other direction, is full of them. I was the only big-nose in town. As such, I had a selfish sense of having the place to myself.
The fact is hilarious to contemplate, but Chongqing has been "twinned" with Toronto, with which it has almost as much in common as it does with its three other unofficial siblings, Toulouse, Seattle, and Hiroshima. It is even difficult to say how big Chongqing is. Chinese policy seems to be to speak of it only in the context of the vast region whose administrative centre it is, an area of nine districts, twelve counties, 2,300 square kilometres, and 14 million people. *The Times Atlas* gives the city's population as 6 million. In fact, the core appears to be a place of a million or two — it's hard to say because the density is so obviously high and the twisting narrow hilly streets, which are far too steep for bicycles, make it difficult to get an overview. More to the point, there is nothing in the least postmodern about it. Chongqing has old-fashioned skyscrapers and streets that are absolutely alive. Stand still for five minutes and you will be passed by women in high-collared and high-slit silk dresses (as though their grandmothers had described how Myrna Loy looked playing Fu Manchu's daughter) and old men carrying coal in baskets suspended from bamboo poles, or soldiers wearing tennis shoes with their uniforms, and people buying and selling rice and wristwatches and furniture and medicines and God knows what all. Everybody is on the move, and on the make, all of the time. The streets are constantly full of honking cars and lorries, but it is the

honking that is extinct everywhere else, which you hear otherwise only on the soundtracks of movies made in the 1940s.

I think that date is significant. It was during the War of Resistance Against Japan that Chongqing entered modern history. Chiang Kai-shek was driven out of Nanjing (Nanking), his original capital, and moved his army and the whole corrupt bureaucracy to Wuhan (Hankou). The Japanese air force and army drove him out of there as well; 300,000 were killed. So he withdrew even deeper in-country. Accordingly it was in Chongqing that the Allies maintained the Far Eastern Division headquarters, and it was at Chongqing that Mao and Chiang forged, or had forced on them, their rather shortlived alliance against the Japanese. Edgar Snow described the city in *Red Star Over China* as a "place of moist heat, dust and wide confusion. . . ." The first day I was there the heat and dust were kept in abeyance by a constant torrential rain, but the wide confusion was still in effect, proving that it exists independent of warfare, which is what Snow was describing.

As much as half of Chongqing was damaged or destroyed by the Japanese; tens of thousands more people were killed. The citizens dug shelters into the sides of the mountain; the shelters are still there and are used as workshops, warehouses, retail stores, in one case as a dance hall. Perhaps even more so than in most other Chinese centres, the people turn all usable space to good account, aided by a degree of new economic freedom not found in many of the other provincial cities. I saw a lot of family-run restaurants with as few as four tables, and other matchbox enterprises. With the rain persisting, I saw one man stick up a light tarpaulin over a little patch of pavement, put an old crate beneath it, and go into business as a barber. On another street was an alfresco pool table, protected by a sheet of heavy PVC, its four corners tied to trees and poles. Precisely because of the people's resilience, it was easy to visualize how Chongqing must have been during the war, when Japanese bombers had only to follow the Yangtze to the peanut-shaped peninsula formed by the confluence of the two rivers. Despite American aid, and in part because of China's own extraordinary systemic corruption at that time, the Kuomintang was sorely pressed for supplies and *matériel*, and the city was only lightly defended against air raids.

The wartime residence of Mao, Zhou Enlai, and other leading communists, called Red Crag Village, was pulled down after the war for a museum to commemorate that which had been razed: the Red Crag Revolutionary Memorial Hall. Chongqing also has a chamber of horrors that tells the story of SACO, the Sino-American Co-operation Agreement, under which Americans trained China's secret police in torture techniques and so on. But that is as much official acknowledgement as Chiang is given. The houses he built for himself and his pro-communist sister-in-law up on the face of Yellow Mountain were handed over to a local hospital as auxiliary space and now are slowly being reclaimed by the rainforest, unmarked and unremarked on. I was determined to visit if I could.

We should have had a Jeep rather than a car to travel the mountain road. For much of the way we inched behind a truck full of armed police. Our driver kept honking at them, which struck me as an imprudent thing to do. The windscreen wipers couldn't begin to deal with the problem of so much rain. Rivers of water were running down the leaves of trees, leaves the size of elephant ears, and falling onto the ones below, so that the whole forest on either side of the road was like some elaborate water clock in the emperor's collection in the Forbidden City.

Near the summit, at an elevation of maybe 600 metres, was a long tropical-style building: the hospital. It seemed deserted except for a few nurses walking along the verandah, unconcerned with the way the rain was blowing in. Chiang's house was farther up still, at the end of a long series of twisting steps cut into the steep side of the mountain. We trudged up, slipping in the mud and soaked to the skin.

The house is sometimes described as a villa by Chinese, but they are using the term in the English sense not the European, to mean a small country house rather than a large luxurious one. Yet in this case the location alone, overlooking the city and the river valley far below, might almost justify the grander usage, though the structure is only a tiny two-storey dwelling, plain but sturdily built, with its own water tower. It is a house that would have been easy to defend, except against an air attack — which was precisely the danger Chiang faced. Accordingly, he used to come here only after dark and always left before daybreak. The sight of his motorcade departing the city became the signal for an exodus in rickshaws, on pack animals, and on foot.

An old man lives there now. He pretty much keeps to the first floor, giving over the ground floor to his chickens and ducks. He sleeps on a cot in what was once the Generalissimo's bathroom, because part of the roof above the bedroom has rotted away, admitting water freely. His possessions include a couple of pots and pans and a few rice bowls. Whatever he cannot grow must be lugged up all the way from the city. Perhaps 100 metres away, along a slippery, overgrown path, is the slightly smaller house built for the U.S. military adviser in the region. It is used for the spillover from the hospital down below. There were only two rooms on the ground floor, one for sleeping and one that served as the war room for strategic conferences and such. In the latter, we found six old women playing dominoes. They seemed surprised by our turning up, our hair like wet seaweed and our boots squeaking. One sensed they had no visitors even in dry weather. We tried to chat them up and soon they were quite jolly about our presence. I got the impression, I'm not sure how exactly, perhaps only from their expressions, that they were tubercular.

When we got back down into the city, traffic was in an even greater snarl than usual. While we were stalled with everyone honking at us and us honking back, I had one of those experiences, so common in China if you are alert to receive them, in which past and present become confused for a second. A man came out of his house, which was perched precariously on a cliff overlooking the Yangtze docks, and held up what looked at first like a bandoleer of rifle cartridges but was actually an enormously long string of firecrackers. With great ceremony he held a lighted match to the bottom end, with results that drowned out the noise of the impatient cars and lorries. It was exactly noon. Someone in his household had died. Each day for three days — perhaps four, if there were relatives who had to travel a great distance to the funeral — he would perform this ceremony at 6 a.m., noon, 6 p.m., and midnight. Then the body would be taken away for disposal.

When I returned to the hotel to put on some dry clothes, the television was showing highlights of the Calgary Stampede in Chinese.

Two of the areas in which I was least ill-equipped to make comparisons between conditions in China and those in the Soviet Union were the press and the fine arts, both quite useful indicators of social health in addition to their other importance. I knew that since the era of reform started ten years ago the *People's Daily* has lost millions of readers, just as *Pravda* has done. I had not been aware of just how the situation had been corrected following the massacre. It seems that as part of the plan to strengthen the party, a certain quota of persons at every factory, office, and neighbourhood committee were required to purchase subscriptions, with the cost subsidized by the state. Beijing actually paying people to read its own newspaper may strike the West as curious, but the policy has apparently had the desired effect.

No one foresees any likelihood that China will allow the type of semi-independent newspapers represented in the U.S.S.R. by the *Moscow News* or *Arguments and Facts*, though *China Daily*, the English-language paper that the party began producing in 1981, comes close to free expression by including material from foreign agencies and publications with government information not commonly available except in this translated form. People say of it what people say of Radio Moscow's English service in contrast to the Russian-language radio and television: that because it is for foreigners it can afford to be more candid or at least much less secretive, putting the best possible face on a situation but not denying that the situation exists. But that is as far as the Chinese and Soviet press might be compared at the present. The *China Daily* — and in this, I am assured, it is just like the Chinese-language media — places an unnatural and not always credible emphasis on good news about production and the economy. One might be tempted to dismiss this practice as universal socialist procedure if not actually attribute it to government manipulation, but I feel the trait may also reflect a basic difference in Chinese culture. Westerners go to China wanting to see ancient temples only to find the Chinese eager to show them hydroelectric projects and ugly sky needles that look like the CN Tower (the Soviet Union is full of them as well). Frustration naturally results. And when the Chinese, in an effort to give the foreign public what it wants, erect brand-new temples in the old style (the original having most likely been destroyed in the Cultural Revolution), the tourists are disappointed and the Chinese hurt and perplexed by such a reaction.

In its way, the press of Chongqing provided an unexpected example of this phenomenon — an unexpectedly pleasant one for me. Zhao Xiaoci, a short, slight middle-aged man with thin spectacles and a quickly energetic manner, took up my presence with enthusiasm. He is chief editor of *Chongqing Daily*, the morning paper, which together with its sister publication, *Chongqing Evening*, and a combined weekly edition for farmers, has a total circulation of about 600,000 copies. He gave me the tour.

When I was there, the newspaper, which I was led to believe rises above standard-issue propaganda only in its local coverage, was in the process of moving to a new plant near the Chaoqian Docks on the banks of the Jialing on the north side of town, though it was still being edited, set, and printed at a rambling complex in Jiefang Lu, on the southern (Yangtze) side of the peninsula. The structures were erected in 1953, the same year that Deng Xiaoping, who was then the party secretary for southwest China, did the calligraphy that is still used in the newspaper's nameplate at the head of page one. They could have been erected in 1923 or 1913. The publisher's office and the conference room were bright, airy, and modern, but the other spaces in the editorial building harked back to another era, one that ended so long ago in western newspapers that it is beyond the reach of even my own elastic recollection. Corridors and cubbyholes were dark and stale-smelling, with brown and yellow paint peeling in leaf-size pieces from the wall. One room was full of reporters with their feet up on the desks, some talking into phones, others pointedly doing nothing. An old girlie calendar hung from one wall. There was, I swear to God, a ceiling fan revolving ever so slowly. The sickly sweet smell of clogged urinals hung in the atmosphere. Many a spavined old hack at the Toronto Press Club would have been quite overcome with nostalgia.

The back shop and the press room were fascinating too. The paper uses an unholy alliance of technologies, both offset and letterpress. No evidence here of the Chinese typewriter invented by Lin Yutang, that remarkable writer about due for revival; copy is written with a pen on graph paper, one character per square. The manuscript pages are then given to young female compositors, twenty-one of them spaced over two shifts, who work not just with the California case familiar to my fellow fogies but sit surrounded by a multitude of cases, with thousands of characters, which they pluck out in proper order and put onto their composing sticks. Excepting the extent of the alphabet the compositors are faced with, the procedures would be instantly familiar to William Lyon Mackenzie or Joseph Howe if those gentlemen could be resurrected to witness the scene. The compositors can set 1,500 characters per hour; the very best might reach a speed of 1,800. There was something wonderfully Dickensian in how they went about the labour, proud of their skill and content with their place in the greater scheme of things.

That realization brought me to another one that affected me very much in Chongqing particularly but everywhere else I went in China as well. The problem with writing about travel in China, I thought — and it applies to all countries that use corrugated iron for roofing material (a distinction I prefer to the term *Third World*) — is that one is constantly coming upon strange sights and ways long lost in the West, which it is too easy to categorize as obsolescent or imitative or backward or otherwise inferior but which one secretly enjoys as proof of one's own now sadly irretrievable past. It is of course a hideous double standard, and generally counter-productive to any understanding of the contemporary scene. But I consoled myself that it is perhaps not completely worthless with respect to the history of China's relations with (or reactions against) the West. To walk into the Bank of China's Chongqing branch is to see two generations of cultural imperialism. Beneath the grime and the half-light and the chaos, all somewhat suggestive of an Indian railway station, is a magnificent old banking hall from the days when banks were designed to convey security and stability rather than convenience. Later it was reclaimed for Chinese culture, but now a new kind of internationalism is making inroads. The woman who waited on me at the foreign exchange wicket sat on a high stool like a Scots clerk in a counting house, and she used an abacus. Above her was a plastic sign reading: "Use 'Great Wall MasterCard' from the Bank of China".

My next call was on Fan Pu, vice-president of the Sichuan Fine Art Institute, the only such place of learning in all of southwestern China and one of only four in the country. He is fifty-six but looks far younger and is himself a painter, or used to be; what with all the administration he looks after, he finds he has little time now for his own work, even on the two one-month holidays, summer and winter. This puts him at a disadvantage in terms of his personal economics as well as his spirit, as he must live on his monthly salary, the equivalent of thirty to fifty dollars, and not supplement it with the occasional sale of works for a couple thousand yuan each, as the other staff, and many of the students, do.

He is from a village in Shanxi in north-central China and fell into art education by way of the military. He was a very young war artist attached to the Eighth Route Army, assigned to paint slogans and such. Later he was involved in an art education programme for the troops generally, which proved to be a springboard to art training after Liberation. A few years later, in 1956, Mao would make one of his better-known pronouncements on the subject: "Let a hundred flowers blossom and let a hundred schools exist." But, in fact, the process was already well underway. The Southwest

People's College of Art had begun in 1950, and in 1953, as part of national "adjustments" in the education system, merged with the Chengdu School of Art to make the Southwest Training College of Art, with the emphasis on turning out teachers. In 1959 the school got its present name to reflect a broader approach. It now has 800 students — 700 of them undergraduates moving towards their state-assigned craft or design jobs once they get their degrees, the rest postgrads hoping to teach one day. There are 200 staff, from full professors to teaching assistants. Most teachers are Sichuan School graduates. The campus is a pleasant enclave of buildings on 11 hectares on the north side of the Yangtze, a surprisingly quiet spot in the middle of such a noisy urban area. The centrepiece is a six-storey sextagonal building with several floors of exhibition space, complete with spittoons in the corners.

Only about one in twenty applicants is accepted as a student, for people wishing to enrol must show at least some ability in most of the major areas of the curriculum, which includes painting (both Chinese and western), drawing, colour theory, and the philosophy of art. Great emphasis is put on the last one. They must also pass the standard exam set by the National Committee for Education in such fields as mathematics, philosophy, politics, and language, though they need achieve a mark of only 200, not 400 as required of students in other fields, at other institutions. I had hoped to meet with the students, but my visit fell on Monday afternoon when they were all away for their weekly dose of political indoctrination, a rite that was reintroduced following Tiananmen Square after many years' absence. Fan was apologetic, but no doubt his superiors scheduled my appointment with this coincidence in mind. In any case, it was impossible not to admire his own adroitness when the subject of politics came up.

Mao had great concern for art education, great plans, Fan insisted, "but these were not implemented till after the Cultural Revolution was finished." Nicely put, I thought. I wondered how the place had survived the wave after wave of carnage, destruction, and mayhem. "The past ten years, however, have been the best and most valuable time we've ever had." The reference was to the Third Plenary of the Central Committee in 1979, which freed artists and art schools from strict adherence to social realism and useful propaganda to pursue whatever might, within reasonable limits, result in "quality".

"Painters enjoy greater freedom now if they're not against the teachings of the Communist Party or of socialism", Fan told me. "On the other hand, no one in my school is against those things, but of course such matters are harder to judge here than at, say, a drama school." He was too subtle to mention it, and I was too polite to bring it up, but each knew that the other knew that the issue was not political content of the art but rather the degree of political correctness inherent in various types of art, quite apart from imagery.

The watershed event in the modern story of free artistic expression in China, an event as important as the Soviet show of "modern" work closed down by Krushchev, was an exhibition at the National Gallery in Beijing little more than a year earlier, right before Tiananmen Square, when the liberalization movement reached its peak. The show was devoted to the work of students from throughout China and featured stuff that would have provoked only ennui in the West. There were a lot of pop images, for example, and large imitation abstract-expressionist canvases onto which the artists had shot paint from a great distance. Found art found expression in such objects as a condom filled with water. The authorities were outraged. The show, which was to have run for a month, closed early. Yet that did not presage a retreat to the bad old days but only an acceptance that western ideas must be assimilated slowly, that new eras should not be entered into until the previous ones have been dissected, digested, and understood. "We try to absorb more western culture" is how Fan put it, "but we don't want to make a copy. We need to consider the condition of China and the customs and to try to absorb quality, whether East or West."

As a result, I got a sense of telescoping time as I wandered through the rooms of the gallery, as though the main purpose of the instruction in art history and technique were to find ways of applying the one to the other. I saw traditional Chinese scroll painting with the unmistakable influence of the Mexican muralists of the 1920s and even some that tried to acknowledge cubism, and one large lacquerware mosaic of a field of flowers that incorporated the vocabulary of pointillism. Sometimes the institute has picked up the least likely of western ideas. Students in the fashion design course, for example, are crazy about 1960s tie-dyeing, which is sometimes used in figurative work; some silk tie-dye pandas by Fan's wife were on display. But then, that seems somehow appropriate. Chinese artists are fighting the battle and making the discoveries that western art worked its way through in the early 1960s. Which in no way makes the issues any less important or the lessons any less real, for the time difference is a vital part of the context needed to decipher such events, which are themselves a useful illustration of changes the larger society is going through.

One of the former students of whom the institute is proudest is Luo Zhonghi, whose 1979 painting "Fathers", a sort of superrealist portrait done in earth colours but with a nod towards neo-expressionism, is considered a masterpiece. It depicts an old farmer holding up a soup bowl or rice bowl, as though offering sustenance to the viewers or begging from them. It was praised by some critics in France when it appeared there in a group show; it now hangs permanently in the National Gallery in Beijing. Its wide acceptance in China would seem to rest on the way it uses a variety of "international" techniques to acceptable documentary ends. Although, despite its descriptive content, it is not what a western audience would immediately think of as overtly socialist art, it is greatly esteemed in China at least partly because it is not considered too western despite its form.

The closest work to this ideal middle ground that I saw on display in the students' gallery was a reclining female nude in the manner that a Canadian viewer might associate with Ken Danby or, more recently, Jeremy Smith. It is the work of a current female graduate student. The faint, very faint, element of eroticism added to the effectiveness of the compromise between mission and explanation. I asked Fan whether there are life classes, thinking that they might have been banished from the syllabus when the recent crackdown came. He said oh yes and mixed classes at that. "But it is hard to find female models. They fear that young men won't want to be their friends if they know that other people have seen them undressed, and this is often the case. We must therefore use girls from the distant countryside, and they are not the best models, they're not trained." Male models do not face the same stigma. But then I should have guessed that life-drawing classes continue to be important. Students at the institute still draw from the antique as well, using copies, made by teachers thirty years ago, of the ancient sculptures from nearby caves. I was reminded of the old copies of Greek and Roman sculpture once used for the same purpose in Moscow but now relegated to display in the Pushkin Museum of Fine Arts in lieu of any genuine classical statuary for the people to look at.

In short, Fan explained, "abstraction moves slowly here", as though abstraction were the one barrier western art has had to break through, as though, now having done so, all is stable and static. "But the students are aggressive." Later he would mention their penchant for long hair, speaking like a Canadian high school principal of twenty-five years ago — "There is a new atmosphere in the school." I got the impression that this new atmosphere might be described as a kind of enlightened pragmatism.

To judge from what I saw, the level of craft in the students' work is quite high and the interdisciplinary breadth remarkable. A person might ultimately specialize in the plastic arts but is expected to have a reasonable grasp of ceramics, or, in a pinch, be able to execute a portrait. This approach is apparently the outcome of several factors. The socialist tradition, for one. Students, and their teachers, do a lot of urban design work and public art. Sichuan graduates worked on Mao's mausoleum, for example, and the sculpture department was responsible for the allegorical sculptures, representing the four seasons, that decorate the approaches to the nearby Yangtze Bridge. Another factor is the deliberate attempt to meld the visual imperative of Chinese art with that of the western modernist tradition. (To this end, incidentally, the institute has often set up exchanges of staff and students with those in Canada, apparently feeling that Canada provides western culture in its least virulent form.) You can see the results of this policy in all but the most traditional work. It is particularly strong in commercial design, which the students undertake for Chinese factories in need of help with their packaging. As the counter-measures imposed after Tiananmen Square ease up (let us hope), and the move towards a more market-driven economy resumes, such skill can only be in even greater demand. That may not have much to do with art, but it is the institute's safe-conduct pass into the future.

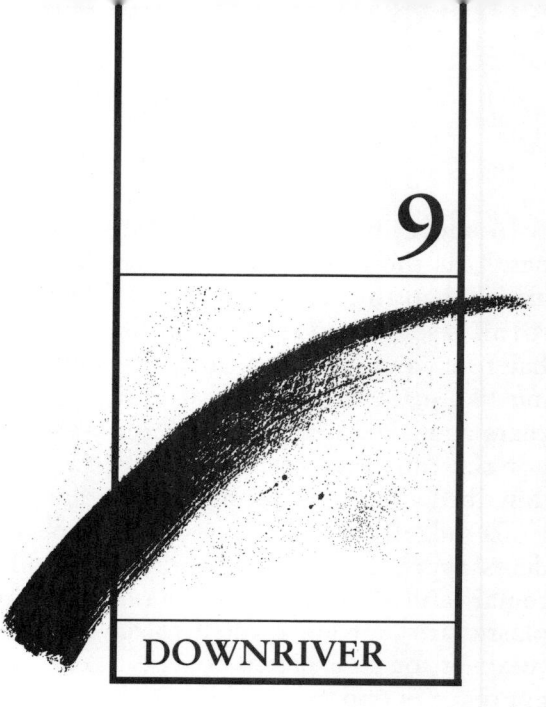

9

DOWNRIVER

Shortly after dawn on the day of departure from Chongqing I stood at the head of the long flight of steps looking down the hill to the Jialing and, beyond it, the Yangtze. There was motion everywhere. Fifty or sixty sizable ships were loading or unloading or criss-crossing their fellow vessels' wakes in the one river or the other — passenger steamers, river freighters, oar-carriers, ferry boats. A few more were careened up on the mud flats where workers were going at them on bamboo scaffolding. In addition, a disorganized flotilla of smaller craft, some with family laundry flapping from the rigging, loitered about, like birds following behind hoping to pick up a little food when the garbage was thrown overboard — or rather, hoping to pick up any spare bits of commerce that the big vessels couldn't be bothered with. Hundreds of people were moving back and forth between the ships and the shore. Many were passengers, others were stevedores and roustabouts. They walked along rickety gangplanks that oscillated alarmingly under the weight. Some carried enormous cloth bundles tied with rope, bundles that dwarfed the people under them and gave the suggestion of ants trying to make off with someone's picnic food. Still others trotted along with wicker baskets on their heads or two of them bouncing suspended from bamboo poles that dug deeply into their shoulders. A number of people appeared to be carrying all their worldly possessions with them — mattresses, cooking utensils, small animals. Children cried, dogs barked, and whistles hooted hoarsely. The New Orleans levee in 1855 cannot have looked or felt much different.

It was time to respond to one of my original motivations in coming to China and begin passage downriver through the Three Gorges, an area only about 200 kilometres in length but possessing some of the most famous scenery in Asia. To get the tickets I had to queue up in an old riverfront terminal where people were sleeping on the hard wooden benches while elderly women fanned themselves and Public Security officers strolled up and down with utterly unconvincing nonchalance, alert to the ways of beggars and pickpockets.

In socialist China there are no first-class cabins. There are entire first-class boats, you see, big sleek motor yachts for the exclusive use of tourists and important officials, where people can sit in swivel chairs in air-conditioned comfort and watch through the glass while the scenery comes to them. Wen Dong and I were going to take one of the hundreds of Chinese boats that go up and down the river. Except that they are steel-hulled and aren't driven by paddlewheels, they look like the old riverboats we associate with the Mississippi or the Yukon — and for a reason. They have the same shallow spoon-shaped hull, drawing only a metre or so of water, in order to glide over incipient sandbars when the river is low. Atop that are three decks, with a sort of parlour forward, on the uppermost one, and the pilot house on what would once have been called the texas deck.

The highest order of accommodation is second class, in which two people — Wen and I in this instance — share a small outward-facing cabin containing a basin, a vacuum bottle of tea water, and two life jackets. The toilets are common to all the second-class passengers and consist of stinking holes in the floor. In third class, one deck below, there are four small chromium-plated bunks to a cabin instead of two single beds, whereas fourth-class, on the waterline, is made up of twenty-four-bunk dormitories. There is also fifth class, below decks, in which people simply sprawl on the steel decking, moaning and tossing like prisoners, without much in the way of light or air but sometimes with a pig or two for additional company (for it is a strict rule — and a sound one, I feel — that all farm creatures must travel fifth class). The uniqueness I had experienced as a westerner in Chongqing was continued aboard ship, as I was again the only foreigner in sight unless you counted a few Taiwanese. The next most exotic person was a wealthy Tibetan. I assume he was wealthy, for all his teeth, uppers and lowers, were of gold. And by comparison he didn't excite much curiosity at all. At 7 a.m. we steamed out into the Yangtze channel and began moving eastward. We were underway. Over the PA system, very loudly, came a recording of "Auld Lang Syne" played on Chinese instruments.

The rains this year were early and determined, and the river was a little higher than usual. It was also, I had pointed out to me, more red than yellow, an indication of the amount of farmland it was taking away with it over its course of 3,600 kilometres. The Yangtze is by far China's largest river and one of the three biggest on the planet, but all other statistics about it incline towards meaningless numbers with many digits. Almost at once, however, I had a sense of its power as a thief, constantly stealing earth where it's most needed and depositing it where it is wanted least, in channels and berths, which then must be dredged, or in new bars and shoals, which pose a hazard to navigation. The government estimated that this year could see the worst flooding on the Yangtze, particularly in the middle ranges, since 1954, when the snows in Tibet were particularly deep and 30,000 people were killed and whole villages destroyed. Even in a good year, 3,000 Chinese are killed in floods.

For the first while beyond Chongqing the view is industrial. The plants look heavy and old-fashioned, but you don't get the sense of industrial autumn you do seeing similar scenes in America or Britain. There is no leading edge to Chinese manufacturing; it simply exists and does its job and keeps its share of the work force busy in the process. Between the industrialized areas are sizable stretches of open country, and as the built-up places get farther apart, the countryside in between becomes both more rugged-looking and more intensively cultivated.

Here, gazing up at the sides of hills and cliffs to find small square vegetable patches, I saw my first examples of the almost completely vertical gardening at which the Chinese excel. In the Soviet Union, I had been surprised to realize to what extent food shortages underlay the urgency of reform. Now I saw the miracle by which the Chinese manage to feed themselves and that gives the government a level of stability that cannot be compared to the Soviets'. I could only guess at all the reasons for the difference, but some are purely practical. In the U.S.S.R. the Stalinist legacy of enormous collective farms for crops like winter wheat and potatoes — crops that more or less take care of themselves between planting and harvest — gave permanence to a serious misapplication of human resources. The Chinese scheme of small communes, often no more than a few families, growing labour-intensive crops like rice, is much more efficient. Although the statement is not terribly scientific, it must also be said that the Russians probably just aren't as good farmers as the Chinese; the Doukhobors seem to have taken their special genius with them when they emigrated. Given controlled conditions and identical adjoining plots in a neutral third country, the Russian would starve and the Chinese would feed an extended family of twenty-three people. What was it Brecht wrote in *Threepenny Opera?* "*Erst Kommt das Fressen, dann Kommt die Moral.*" First food, then morals. A lot of other words could be substituted for *Moral* without altering the meaning.

We passed a number of villages that would have reminded Mark Twain of his boyhood in Hannibal: towns with only a few streets, all of them running parallel to the muddy river, where people seemed willing to interrupt their work and watch, with what combination of emotions I could hardly imagine, whenever a riverboat like ours chugged by without stopping — rather as I had observed people doing in the case of the Trans-Siberian train.

Before noon we came to the first sizable city, called Fuling, which looks like one of the villages that long ago had been multiplied in size by the addition of industry. The river there is full of rocks and whaleback shoals, which must be major protrusions indeed when the water is low. It is also particularly dirty along this stretch, with bottles and every other form of rubbish floating by, including polystyrene packaging and other permanent waste. Such conditions seem to have no noticeable effect on the people whose lives are spent along the river. At almost every bend for the next two days we saw lone fishermen perched on smooth rocks near the bank, casting huge conical nets attached to long poles, and small individual fishing boats with women sitting on deck, mending nets. Sometimes there were hawks circling overhead. The river had been up to one and a quarter kilometres wide, but at about 2 p.m. it suddenly narrowed for a brief stretch and grew rougher, as though to remind us that we were on the right course if we intended to pass through the gorges the next day. It is near here that China may one day build the Three Gorges Dam, a structure 200 metres high that would create a reservoir an estimated 400 kilometres long, flooding a vast inhabited area, including entire cities, and dispossessing millions of people. The project was proposed in the 1950s; the most recent stage is yet another feasibility study, this one partly funded by the Canadian government.

The hills here are very high — as much as 500 metres in some places, I would guess. They are covered in vegetation of different textures, from the leafy to the woolly, and painted many shades of green. The summits are often decorated with a fringe of mountain foliage, while close to the river the style is more subtropical, with elongated fronds overhanging the water. At a distance, the steep face of the hills sometimes looks like green velour. High up there were periodical flashes of silver, as the sun caught waterfalls that make their way down the rocks in a series of graduated leaps before spilling quietly into the river.

The buildings we passed along the way are usually situated on narrow shelves notched into the hillside for that purpose, but the architecture is surprisingly varied. In the countryside, farmers build and own their own houses, unlike people in the towns and cities, where all real property is held in common by the state and assigned for use according to complicated formulae that meet with few people's complete satisfaction. These farmhouses are usually a single storey consisting of two or three rooms; no two are of precisely the same plan, though all seem to be built sturdily and with great vernacular skill. In some cases, local brick is used. Certain people have elected, or been permitted, to settle off by themselves, surrounded by their own kitchen- and market-gardens, while other houses have grown up in clusters, no doubt through the dictates of family need. I saw several instances of what first appeared, from upriver, to be a lone house near a stream but turned out, as we passed, to be only the most visible part of a village strung out along the shores of the tributary for what looked like some considerable distance. Each such place would be governed, some might say ruled, by the rural equivalent of the neighbourhood committees that are the dominant feature of life in the big cities.

Perched up in the hills were two or three impressive temples and also many larger residences with their own boat slips or even their own private docks down below, reached by stone steps or a smooth, steep span of roadway or some combination of the two. As with so many buildings in China, it is impossible to tell what they once must have been or how old they are or even what purpose they are put to now. It seemed to me, though, that some had walls that went beyond the needs of the traditional Chinese courtyard to suggest fortification. And it was brought home to me that although virtually the entire Yangtze valley was de facto a ~~protectorate~~ COLONY of the British, who kept it so with a fleet of gunboats named for various species of English birds, this countryside, and indeed much of China, was in the hands of warlords as recently as fifty years ago. Perhaps such thoughts came more easily to mind aboard a riverboat like ours. A tablet affixed to one of the bulkheads informed me that the boat was launched in 1981, but to judge by the design, the rust, the battered wooden doors, and the general signs of rough handling, it might just as easily have been built in 1921.

Our boat was never alone on the river for long. Downwardbound vessels naturally have the right of way, and we forever seemed to be passing, or being passed by, other identical ones, always with an exchange of whistle blasts. Also, there were work boats galore, from two-person fishing craft of four metres or less to more substantial wooden-hulled affairs that were probably operated by communes and used to deliver crops to market. At one place where the channel hugged the north bank we passed close enough to a boat slip to see that it was rice that the long line of men were carrying aboard in slow, methodical single file. Usually we could only guess at what cargo was being carried, except of course in the case of unpackaged commodities. Salt and tung oil are two common cargoes, but coal was the most obvious. All along the river, as far as we went, there were coal mines close to the shore. Some were so small that they seemed to be worked by only a handful of men; in one instance, the coal was being dug out of the hillside and shovelled directly into the belly of a waiting scow. In other cases, miners underground sent it up by lift, tram, or conveyor, building up huge stockpiles on the surface, which other men would transfer to wheelbarrows and push along a wobbly tipple before dumping the coal into the vessel perhaps 25 metres below. It must take forever to fill the three holds of a respectable-sized ship of the sort that carries on most such trade between Shanghai and all manner of little places up the river.

Towards late afternoon we put into Fengdu on the northern bank. The procedure for tying up at such cities is to come abreast of a barge with a high superstructure that is permanently moored to the dock; each barge bears a number corresponding to that of the particular boat it services. The barge thus acts as a kind of bridge between the life on the river and the life in town. As soon as the deckhands have secured the boat to it with hawsers, the barge comes to life. Even before the gangplank is put in place, men and women on the barge are selling to the passengers sodas and packets of dried beef and pieces of some rubbery white vegetable, passing the goods and making change over a gap of slurping water. The stops last only a few minutes, just long enough to discharge some people and take on others, but folks are eager to step onto land again and they penetrate as far into town as they can before the all-aboard bell calls them back. The townspeople know they have to conduct their trade swiftly.

The street nearest the dock is always a miniature market for those who can afford to buy food for the next leg of the journey. There is a restaurant of sorts below deck, in the fifth-class section, but the food is slop (I never thought I'd ever say that about what is basically Cantonese cooking — we had now gone beyond the jurisdiction of Sichuan cuisine, though Sichuan accents, which are almost equally spicy, were still common enough). The diners huddle together at small tables and sit on square handmade stools about 30 centimetres off the ground. There were more people than stools and fisticuffs broke out between two patrons, both of whom had the look of street toughs. Police ride all the boats as a matter of routine, and a Public Security officer broke up the dispute before the violence became general.

The channel is well marked and well monitored. There are frequent stations along the way where conditions are checked and information disseminated; these facilities are housed in red-and-white buildings with flagpoles out front and with depth markers painted on the rocks leading up the hillside. Despite that, rocks, sandbars, logs and other obstacles, and even occasional wrecks, make night travel impossible. It would certainly be foolhardy to attempt a nocturnal passage of the gorges, where the water levels can vary as much as 25 or 30 metres according to the season. So at seven o'clock we tied up for the night at Wanxian, an old city on the north bank with a wide stone staircase leading up from the dock into the commercial section, where a market is conducted after dark more for the benefit of the citizens than for the passengers. In other words, it is not primarily a market for crafts and packaged food but for furniture and clothing and housewares as well, though any Chinese market, in however provincial a town, has enough fresh meat and produce to provoke food riots in the Soviet Union.

Wanxian is another of those cities along the river that benefited from the British ability to get trading concessions in the confusion of the last days of the Manchu dynasty — or, in this case, in the early moments, equally chaotic, of the Chinese Republic, in the idealistic period before Sun Yat-sen's death opened the way for Chiang Kai-shek; there are still old buildings that don't require plaques to tell the story. The city has a couple of hundred thousand inhabitants at least, tightly packed into a small space, as the contours of the river and mountains insist. It is big enough and busy enough to suggest a need for traffic signals; the total absence of any such devices increases not only the congestion but also the sense of excitement, the realization that what you are seeing is the urban experience, Chinese style.

We were underway again at first light, and within an hour the river had started to boil and churn. But this was only another of the signposts along the route. When it finally began, Qutang, the shortest and swiftest of the gorges, came up suddenly and was over too soon but really was magnificent while it lasted. We had two more towns to pass before the ride could begin — Fengjie, not far from the head of the gorge, and then Baidicheng, or White King City, a place whose mythical associations are buried now in coal yards and boat yards. This whole part of the valley is particularly rich in archaeological sites, including some dating to the Stone Age, for that is how long the river has been sustaining people here. We made our way into the canyon, which is only eight kilometres long, playing tag with other boats. The experience is a bit like being on a rollercoaster that never leaves the ground, but with high stone walls racing past on both sides.

The second gorge, called the Wuxia, is more dramatic and more than twice as long. The mountains remind you of photographs of the Andes perhaps, with the tops in cloud cover. Right in the middle of the gorge is a town called Badong, where it must be difficult landing under certain conditions. The vegetation along that section was markedly different from what I had seen the previous day, with more conifers, and I began to notice a difference in the rocks as well: high white shale cliffs rose along one section, with a wavy fern-like pattern to them.

Thereafter the river widens for quite a spell and grows calmer. We saw butterflies in profusion for a few moments and could hear birds chirping, could in fact eavesdrop on the conversation of men in sampans and small motor launches a considerable distance away. This went on for some while until, midafternoon, we entered Xiling Gorge, the last and longest. It runs for about 80 kilometres, not roaring or bubbling but sending the boat along at a fast steady pace, past rock formations riddled, high and low, with caves, some of them quite large and some, it is said, used throughout ancient times by successive cultures. Such matters are of little interest to most Chinese. It is perhaps significant that although the gorges have generated attention abroad, the real excitement for most of the passengers came only later, when the boat passed the huge power station connected to the Gezhouba Dam, a famous Chinese megaproject of which everyone remains most proud. It was begun on December 26, 1970, Mao's seventy-seventh birthday, and opened to the public in 1981. The boats here must pass through a lock, which they do four at a time. Crowds of people atop the lock stare down excitedly as the passengers stare up in turn at the manmade wonder. The people on one boat call out to those on the others. Cameras appear and everyone is happy, awestruck by the majesty of — Progress!

After the dam, the river quickly returns to its broad, muddy, moderately paced old self, and the mundane nature of Chinese country life envelops people once again. Paul Theroux took the inaugural run of one of the first-class tourist boats in the early 1980s, producing a small gem of a book, *Sailing through China*, one of his most satisfying efforts. He hit upon a striking truth when, in watching this part of the river float by, he observed:

> Our future is this mildly poisoned earth and its smoky air. We are in for hunger and hard work, the highest stage of poverty — no starvation, but crudeness everywhere, clumsy art, simple language, bad books, brutal laws, plain vegetables, and clothes of one colour. It will be damp and dull, like this. It will be monochrome and crowded — how could it be different? There will be no star wars or galactic empires and no more money to waste on the loony nationalism in space programmes. Our grandchildren will probably live in a version of China. On the dark brown banks of the Yangtze the future has already arrived.

Travellers have the option of continuing for three more days, to Wuhan, where they can take another boat all the way to Shanghai. I was eager to get to Shanghai more quickly, because it was another of my must-sees and because I had begun to sense that the authorities didn't want me to get there at all, for they had been hinting, suggesting, and inveigling me to change my itinerary in favour of Guangzhou (Canton). I could only guess that they feared I would ferret out some radical democrats in the former place. But I remained determined to get there if only to see the old foreign concessions and other surviving evidence of past clashes between Chinese and western cultures. A compromise was reached. I would go to Shanghai, but quickly, and not stay long, and they would continue to argue in favour of Guangzhou (which, I told them, I could visit anytime on a daytripper's visa from Hong Kong).

I talked with various people on the boat. There was an electronics student, twenty-two, in whose eyes I could see vital questions she wanted to ask about politics in the West but was too frightened to say out loud. And there was a chemical salesman, in his mid-forties, who was still shaking his head in disbelief at what the post-Tiananmen crackdown had done to his state-controlled company. "We were still making the transition to the market economy and I was building up our overseas business", he said. "Then suddenly all that we had built was torn down and we were back to central planning." His expression and the motion of his shoulders said: "It's crazy! Nobody can work like this."

We got off at Yichang, a place that is said to be the throat between the head of Hubei and the stomach of Sichuan. The phrase has a smooth tourist-board sound to it, but there are complicated emotions beneath the surface. The locals speak with something very close to the Sichuan dialect. They deeply resent, however, not being thought of as citizens of Hubei. This is another old treaty port that once had a large British community, then almost totally lost touch with the West, and the West with it. "Before 1970," I was told, "many people here had never actually seen big-noses." That was the year when almost everything in Yichang started to change. Work on the dam and the lock had begun. Then, the next year, a long railway-and-highway bridge across the Yangtze was opened, based apparently on the one completed at Wuhan a dozen years earlier. The Wuhan bridge was the first Chinese-built span to cross the river, for although Chinese bridge engineering had once been quite advanced (Peter the Great summoned Chinese experts to St. Petersburg), it atrophied after the foreigners came in great numbers. The pre-Gezhouba population of Yichang (which got a modern port in the bargain) was 170,000; now the city has 400,000, though like all Chinese cities it looks smaller than it is.

Wen and I barely had enough time to catch our CAAC flight to Wuhan, assuming that the flight still existed and that it hadn't been unreasonably delayed. This entailed a wild ride from the riverfront to the airport over a temporarily unpaved road filled with holes the size of small bomb craters. Prosperous commercial Yichang is only a few streets deep. The rest is like rural China plunked down in the middle of an urban area. Housing ranges from mud buildings at the low end to modern blocks of flats at the high, with the mean being quite adequate. I didn't see as much evidence of economic freedom for small entrepreneurs as I had in other cities. People grow rice and cotton, and I saw others flailing grain — with wooden flails, I mean — and using round baskets to separate out the chaff. There were water buffalo — morose creatures they are — being coached through the paddies, a sure sign that although I was still on the north side of the river I had crossed some other no doubt invisible boundary into southern China. By passing convoys of soldiers and honking at deaf animals and endangering people on bicycles, hazy figures encased in clouds of dust, we managed to get within sight of the airport. A field near by was littered with the hulks of DC-3s and other vintage aircraft. We made it to the terminal with moments to spare before we began a long wait for the plane. On previous CAAC flights we had been given perfectly adequate box lunches. I was ready for another. This time they gave us fans made of sandalwood.

The Canadian embassy in Beijing had told me there were reports of anti-Canadian sentiment in Wuhan; I didn't catch details, but *immigration* and *Vancouver* seemed to be the key words. To people who reached their majority during the Pearson era, the whole notion has an absurd ring. One might as well speak of demonstrations against the Swiss, or of anti-Belgian riots. But times change, which is to say they deteriorate, and I kept my ears and eyes open over the next couple of days but heard or saw nothing to report. If my presence wasn't enough to provoke backlash, I reasoned, there was likely no merit to the story. Yes, I felt myself starting to become just the slightest bit paranoiac by this stage. Nothing clinical, you understand, merely defensive; I almost thought it might be expected of me, and I had no wish to appear rude.

At Wuhan the Yangtze is much wider and slower than it is at Chongqing, and the bridge does add a note of dignity. Wuhan is also bigger and more up to date than Chongqing, though its contemporariness is not the source of whatever charm and interest it possesses. It has quite a bustling indoor-outdoor market along Thousand Families Street, full of the customary snake sellers, dog-meat merchants, kerbstone physicians, key-cutters, and people with medical scales offering to tell you your weight for only a few fen. All this is in addition to packaged goods ranging from wart-remover to Fancy-Smell Biscuits. This was the only market at which I saw people with bamboo beds slung from wires above their stalls so they could sleep there as well as do business. This may — or may not, I couldn't determine — be related to the fact that Wuhan is not so commercially free as it was before Tiananmen; new confiscatory taxes are all but wiping out the entrepreneurs' profit. Yet there is still prosperity to be had for the shopkeeper there, a fact most obvious in, for example, the many electronics dealers' and clothing stores in Dr Sun Yat-sen Street, which looks and feels remarkably like Charing Cross Road in London.

A lot of history shows through in Wuhan, though it is little enough considering the past the place has had. Wuhan is actually three cities joined under a single municipal government for administrative reasons, though the components stubbornly retain their distinct identities. Their functions overlap a bit, but the pattern is for Wuchang, once a walled city, to be the political and cultural centre, while Hankou, where the foreign concessions were, is mostly for shopping, and Hanyang for the most part industrial — famously so. The first of these is on the east side of the river, the others on the west.

Wuhan has often been at the centre of important events. You see that by the presence of more foreign buildings than in either Chongqing or Yichang, though not so many that its character is defined by them, the way Shanghai's is. It was here that the revolution of 1911, ending 267 years of the Qing dynasty, had its beginning. This was also the first part of China to see massive industrialization on the western model and also therefore the first western-style labour violence. The Nationalists took it over, the Japanese seized it and destroyed much of it, and Mao, for some reason, had a special affection for it. It was to Wuhan that he would come annually, until well into his sunset years, to show his strength by swimming in the Yangtze. He was also, it is said, particularly fond of one local restaurant, the Laotongcheng.

It would be inaccurate to say that Wuhan staggers under all that historical baggage. The main sites to which visitors are dragged are a Russian-built hotel in imitation of the Temple of Heaven and a huge five-storey ersatz Buddhist temple completed in the mid-1980s on a high promontory overlooking the bridge approaches and the river. In the morning when I went out, a platoon of soldiers with automatic weapons was doing close-order drill in front of the hotel; they were still at it when I returned in the evening. And if the temple is full of only sham Buddhism, there is genuine peace to be found elsewhere. Wuhan University in

Hankou is one of China's oldest and most important and has an ivy-league sort of campus, belying the violence that erupted there during the Cultural Revolution. I strained to hear indications that today's students are under special suspicion, the way those in Shanghai and particularly Beijing are, but I picked up no such vibrations. It is a well-behaved place, Wuhan. The newspaper has a brand-new office building and printing plant. "That shows how powerful they are", I was told.

Another peaceful spot in the city is East Lake, a large lakeside park with nature paths and some surprisingly quaint amusements, such as shooting galleries, a small private-sector zoo under canvas, and the Chinese equivalent of a Punch and Judy show. On a slow weekday, people can walk there with thoughts disturbed by nothing more jarring that the discontinuous tinkling of bicycle bells, one of the pervasive and characteristic sounds of China.

10
THE BUZZ ON THE SHANGHAI BUND

When I arrived, bedraggled and fatigued, there were two signs, one on either side of the lift, in the lobby of the Peace Hotel in Shanghai, the lovely old Peace Hotel of so many people's warm recollection. One informed patrons that the staff are renowned for their clean linen and attention to personal hygiene. The other said: "Due to necessary renovations, the jazz band which normally is to be found in our lobby may now be heard on the eighth floor temporarily. Our apologies for any inconvenience. You are thanked."

I wanted to stay there because the Peace is of some importance in the history of Shanghai's involvement with the West (and Shanghai was and in one sense remains the most westernized city in China). The story is so fiercely complex that readers new to the subject might not be annoyed by a thumbnail sketch.

Everywhere I went on this journey I am describing I was plagued by anniversaries of this or that war or founding father, all of them dates put on the calendar for immediate political purposes. During my time in China, schoolchildren in Tianjin, Shanghai, and Nanjing were being prepared for celebrations marking the sesquicentennial of the start of the Opium Wars. The conflict had its origin in the late eighteenth century, when factors of the East India Company [BRITISH] began paying for Chinese tea and silk in opium rather than with silver. The opium, most of it from India, was so cheap that the British could afford to dump it on the Chinese market, causing widespread addiction and thus increasing demand. In all, 4,000 chests of opium were imported in 1800, the year the emperor tried banning the stuff (the edict had no effect — even his court was hooked). By 1821, the annual figure was 21,000 chests. In time, the administrator of Canton took it upon himself to close down the opium dens in the city, burn stockpiles of the drug, and behead Chinese traffickers. In 1840, the British fought the first skirmishes to protect the trade. By 1842, they had defeated the Chinese government and forced China to empty the treasury, cede Hong Kong, and grant concessions in various other cities. [DEMOCRACI] These cities became free ports of a kind, in which the British built their own institutions and conducted trade immune from Chinese law. Their success sparked other opium wars on the part of the French, the Americans, the Japanese, the Russians, and others, all of whom also exercised their extraterritoriality, as it was called. Shanghai, as China's biggest port, was at the centre of such activity.

The fourth and final opium war was concluded in 1860, which was a crucial year also because it marked the date when the West finally made up its mind about whom to support in the Taiping Rebellion, a massive peasant uprising led by one Hong Xiuquan, who believed himself to be not the resurrected Christ but rather His younger brother.

Preaching a kind of Christianity and promising land redistribution and other social reforms, including a ban on opium, he put together an army of well over a million and took control of the Yangtze valley and in fact all of southern China. If *war* seems too grand a word for the opium wars, then *rebellion* is too mean a one for the Taiping Rebellion, which claimed millions of lives. The already demoralized Qing government was on the defensive, and the West hesitated whether to support Beijing or wait until the fighting stopped to endorse the Taipings. Finally they came down on the side of the Qings and helped to defeat the rebels; Hong killed himself when cornered, and the threat collapsed. It was in this action that Chinese Gordon acquired his sobriquet — though his greatest fame lay a generation in the future, when he let himself be martyred in Khartoum by the Madhi, another such messianic leader, who claimed to be the Prophet Mohammed returned to Earth and who preached his own kind of anti-foreign message.

With the Taipings vanquished, the westerners now tightened their control even more, perhaps making inevitable the Boxer uprising at the close of the century when another peasant movement based on xenophobia formed an unlikely alliance with the empress dowager to drive the foreigners out. The most dramatic incident in the Boxer conflict, one much beloved by Hollywood and by patriotic illustrators of the Frederic Remington type, was the siege of the foreign legations in Beijing, with a multinational relief force of British, Americans, Japanese, and Europeans coming to the rescue. After that, a few warlords and pirates notwithstanding, the British and others enjoyed clear commercial sailing until the Japanese and then finally the communists expelled them.

In the 1920s and 1930s, Shanghai was fully deserving of its reputation for wickedness and intrigue, but these qualities were not limited to westerners except in the sense that the city was divvied up geographically between Chinese and foreigners. Because it was the place where Chinese sovereignty was most laughable, it was where Chinese dissent was loudest, a city full of revolutionaries and political philosophers. André Malraux is too out of favour even to qualify as a writer who is neglected, but I have always thought that his novel *La condition humaine* must be pretty authentic in the way it describes this underground milieu. It was in Shanghai, in 1921, that the Chinese Communist Party was founded. And it was in Shanghai, in 1927, that Chiang finally turned on the communists, in the celebrated coup and massacre that Malraux describes. The spark was the discovery in the French Concession of a large arms cache that had been confiscated from one of the warlords. The Green Gang, or Green Circle, the organized crime ring that ran most everything in Shanghai that wasn't already run by the foreigners, wanted the guns for its own purposes. The communists, who by that date controlled the labour unions, had plans for them as well. One source says that to even enter Shanghai, Chiang had had to pay tribute to one of the Green leaders, who was driven through the streets in a bullet-proof limousine with gun-toting outriders hanging on the running boards. But Chiang made an alliance with him over the guns. They were two of a kind.

The city now has 6 or 7 million people, the district twice that number. It is a simple matter to divide it into three parts, one might almost say into three levels of consciousness.

First is the foreigners' Shanghai of old, consisting of the former International Settlement and the Bund with its famous skyline, which represents early modernism at its most self-caricaturing, like Buffalo's before urban renewal ruined it or like that of Gotham City in the original *Batman*. The skyscrapers still stand shoulder-to-shoulder alongside the bend in the Huangpu (Whangpoo) River. But the Hongkong and Shanghai Bank at No. 18 has been turned into government offices, and the British consulate at No. 33 has become the Friendship Store, and the Shanghai Club, which claimed to have the longest bar in the world and stood in snooty opposition to the Cercle Sportif Français, was transformed into, of all things, a hostel for Chinese seamen.

Bund is the old Anglo-Indian term for an earthen dike or levee. Its use is fitting in that this was the stronghold of the British imperial presence, though any discussion of the foreigners' quarter must also include the quite separate French Concession, of Frenchtown, and some of the other foreign enclaves. While it lasted, the foreigners' Shanghai was a community of a few hundred thousand set inside the worlds' sixth-largest city, a kind of multicultural canton (no pun intended) where the various language groups mixed with one another as well as with the natives but operated pretty much as they pleased. To quote a 1934 guidebook: "The entertainment is variegated, a Hawaiian hula, Russian mazurka, Parisian apache, negro musicians, Siberian acrobats, London ballroom exhibitionists, American jazz, the Carioca, the tango, the 'dancing hostess'. Ah!" Originally, most of the dancing hostesses were White Russians, an ethnic group conspicuous even in a Shanghai with its 20,000 European Jews, 25,000 Japanese, uncountable British, Americans, French, Belgians, Brazilians, Danes, Swedes, Spaniards, Italian, Dutch — and who knows how many of those curious and wonderful people (I'm always attracted to them) who appear to be all nationalities and none in particular, who seem to speak every living language and accept every currency at par, without fuss or ostentation. Of all the foreigners, only the Russians, Germans, Austrians, and Hungarians were subject to Chinese law.

The guidebook to which I refer has a few ads for doctors who specialized in venereal diseases and many for nightclubs. Sometimes the copy is quite revealing. When you read that the Canidrome Ballroom ("The Rendezvous of Shanghai's Elite") was featuring music by Buck Clayton and his Harlem Gentlemen, you get a pretty clear picture of what passed for sophistication in that time and place — and what didn't register as racism. By comparison, the Ambassador Ballroom in the avenue Edouard 7e in Frenchtown, where "Shanghai's boasted Night Life is at its gayest", promised "100 of the prettiest dancing hostesses for your entertainment". Not to be confused with the Majestic Café, which trumpeted "100 charming dance hostesses". In any case, 100 was clearly the magic number, as it also was for the Shanghai Secondhand Store, whose proprietors could "command the resources of over 100 of the leading pawnshops in Shanghai" and so offer "bargains in rare jewellery, curios which have been the proud possessions for many generations of aristocratic families. . . ."

The whole concept of foreignness, of being a foreigner in a place one has been taught to consider inferior, runs through the book like a red line. Readers are given a quick lesson in pidgin ("Catchee one piece rickshaw" means "Get me a rickshaw") but are warned not to insult well-spoken Chinese with such talk. The Palais Café, "Shanghai's premiere Cabaret [which] with its host of dancing partners and Peppy dance music is THE place for an EVENING of fun", unwittingly summed up what must have been the prevailing attitude when it announced the three foundations on which its business was based: "High Class Drinks. Good Service. Foreign Management."

Ah.

Seldom can such a hopeless place have been so hopeful, and it is in connection with such contradictions that the Peace Hotel fits so snugly. It occupies both sides of the

Nanjing Road, formerly the main street of the British settlement, at right angles to the Bund. Actually it is two hotels now merged into one. The Palace, a four-storey red-brick building, was built in 1903. It is still somehow splendid but now rather cheap, a single renting for only US$32 per night. Almost 60 per cent of the rooms are retained permanently by foreign companies, for what made the location so desirable in the old days — its proximity to the British banks and trading houses — still applies insofar as Chinese banks and trading houses are concerned; the attraction can only grow if Shanghai's new rah-rah mayor succeeds in his plans to have foreign financial institutions and insurance companies readmitted to the Bund. Opposite is the younger, taller, grander former Cathay Hotel, opened in 1929. When it was still brand new, and still the last word, Noel Coward put up there and wrote *Private Lives* in a suite with a sweeping view of the Bund. I prevailed on the good-natured manager to let me into the room with his pass-key; the space has been remodelled almost out of existence, but the panorama remains, with a limitless crush of humanity immediately below the windows. Back in Kingston, Michael Davies had told me of the stares he had received walking along the Bund in a white linen suit (and a reddish beard he sported at the time). I found out what he meant. In fact, the only hostility I felt directed at me anywhere in China was from young men who stared with genuine hatred as I strolled along the Bund — ironically, the spot in all China with the greatest claim on cosmopolitanism and hence, or so one would hope, on tolerance as well.

Several young Chinese I spoke with said that they know next to nothing about pre-liberation Shanghai, only that it was wild and famously sinful. "We were not even taught that much but have learned it from outside school", one explained. They were curious for more, and so I found myself in the unlikely position of telling them about their city. I tried to explain what the European buildings were supposed to represent in European terms — what Threadneedle Street and Lombard Street meant, for example — of how, for all its wide-open atmosphere, there was a countervailing if not very important element of community pride and boosterism. There were protests and demonstrations in 1932, for example, over the opening of Josef Von Sternberg's film *Shanghai Express*, in which Marlene Dietrich utters the imperishable line, "It took more than one man to change my name to Shanghai Lily."

Such is the commercial past. The commercial present, while less romantic, is considerably more pleasant. The communists had a formidable job making Shanghai work again after Liberation. When they took over they found 30,000 prostitutes and probably the most extensive drug addict population in the world at that time. Another legacy was balkanization. The foreigners' Shanghai was so divided that each nationality operated its own dairy, not trusting the other people's milk in a place where lack of pasteurization posed a health hazard, though hardly on the scale of cholera and typhoid. Even forty years later, the city is a maze of twenty-four different standards for sewer systems and electricity grids. Of course, this must also be another example of how the Chinese both embrace and reject change. A further instance would be how Shanghai's night soil is still collected in the traditional manner even though it is no longer used by nearby farmers, who unfortunately have switched to chemical fertilizers.

If it is true to say, as I believe it is, that not even the Cultural Revolution, reign of terror though it was, was able to extinguish the spark of life in Shanghai, it is equally true to say that Shanghai returned the favour by showing communism at its most workable and liveable. This second level of Shanghai consciousness is best seen along the stretch of Nanjing Road from the Bund to Nanjing Xilu, the former Bubbling Well Road, a stretch once associated with night-clubs and coffin-makers' premises but now the main shopping and business street. Nowhere else in China are people so stylishly dressed, nowhere else is such a variety of consumer goods available (a high percentage of them Shanghai-made, with electronics gear being particularly conspicuous). Only Canton has more to offer in this regard, but so much of what it buys and sells originates in Hong Kong.

In the old days there were four famous department stores in Shanghai. They are still there, with new names. They can be recommended for the sceptical (but certainly not for the claustrophobic): everything is available all the time but everybody is grabbing for it all the time as well. From certain angles, this chic and brightly lit part of downtown Shanghai resembles a vast and infinitely more complex version of Montreal — except that the signs are in English.

Shanghai has always been the place to honour the past while experimenting with the future. In Shanghai it is always the Year of the Horse. Pedicabs were introduced in 1926 and within a generation they had doomed the rickshaw. Similarly, today you see only a few junks, unlike ten years ago and unlike present-day Hong Kong. You do, however, spot former junks, with their high sterns cut down; the last ones probably won't disappear for a decade or more. That is the normal pace of Chinese progress, but in Shanghai time generally passes a little more quickly. It is now one of several cities with a stock exchange (a misnomer; so far, trading is mostly in government bonds) and has more automobiles than anyplace else in China and, what is perhaps more telling, more telephone pagers for businessmen (more than 30,000 and climbing quickly). To ride down the river the 25 kilometres or so to where the brown Huangpu meets the yellow Yangtze is to get a sense of what all the commerce is about. For more than an hour you pass a solid row of deep-water shipping, some naval, such as the destroyer escorts and even a few old submarines, but mostly merchant vessels of every description, not only Chinese but incoming ones of many flags. People are quick to say that the citizens of Shanghai are less outward-looking now than the Cantonese, who can stay in touch with the West through Hong Kong, but the difference between the new commercial Shanghai and the pre-Liberation one — aside from a great increase in moral restraint, that is — is that the former was copied from other cultures and the latter is sui generis.

The Chinese leadership wants slow, steady economic change but with political sameness. Sometimes the two policies come together. After Tiananmen Square, the government began punishing urban residents by making them take a portion of their salary in five-year bearer bonds — in effect, imposing a pay cut while raising money for various modernization schemes. Comparisons with the Soviets and with Eastern Europe are inevitable but maybe almost without much value. The two socialisms were always different enough to deny logical collation as well as to preclude co-operation between them. Shanghai seems poised to take advantage of whatever improvements might come, and equally to endure whatever repercussions might follow a renewal of the pro-democracy agitation. One never knows what might happen following the death of the aged Deng Xiaoping. One has no way of knowing which rumours might be true. Did the government really execute a number of generals following the generals' massacre of the students? Or is the Red Army the real secret power now, with the party little more than a shell? Whatever happens, life in Shanghai doesn't actually seem too bad, not as contrasted to its previous recorded high and not as compared with the rest of urban China .

The third Shanghai is the residential one that lies behind the glitter, far from the banks of the Huangpu. There is much that remains to give the feel of an old Chinese city, even if some of it includes western buildings. Life in the lanes and back streets is earthy but not squalid. Apartments are small, even smaller than in Beijing, and one of the common sights is families drying their laundry by putting bamboo poles through the sleeves and leg-holes of their clothes and then shoving the poles out the window until the streets seem to be bizarrely decorated for some holiday.

Daily life for most people is given shape by two bureaucracies, the cradle-to-grave paternalism of the factory (odd how much Chinese socialism resembles Japanese capitalism in this respect) and the equally intense pressure of the neighbourhood committee, whose members, sometimes distinguished by the armbands they wear, keep business hours in small storefront offices that you can recognize without being able to read the signs. Much in people's lives depends on their personal relations with the members as well as on the luck of the draw, but I was told that the neighbourhood committees in Shanghai are generally liberal and understanding, if not as compared with those in Guangzhou then certainly alongside Beijing's or the rural equivalents. I was told of a woman who recently had gone before the committee to seek permission to conceive her one allotted child. She was told that the timing was poor, for the neighbourhood had already exceeded its quota; she would have to wait. She then confessed that she had fibbed a bit. She was already pregnant and had come forward on the assumption that it would be easier to secure permission than to obtain forgiveness (my own experience of bureaucracies suggests precisely the reverse). Normal practice would have been to order an abortion — though others denied this when I repeated the story later. Instead, the committee managed to barter some perk it had lying about for one of the unused pregnancy authorizations of a committee a few streets distant, and no one was any the wiser. At age one and a half, the child will be sent to a sort of day-care centre.

Abortion, as in the Soviet Union, is free and requires no one else's permission but the woman's. But unlike the Soviet Union, China has other forms of birth control. Condoms are free in factories or may be purchased in chemists' shops; in Shanghai, two local firms manufacture them. Compared with repressed Beijing, social life is easy there. The shoppers and office workers are gone from the Bund at night and replaced by strolling lovers. Not far away in Nanjing Road is a news kiosk that even the most unobservant passerby can see is the local meeting place for gays.

Everywhere I went in China I got some sense that the level of religious activity permitted locally was another small indication of the amount of freedom in people's lives. In this respect no place was freer than Shanghai. I couldn't help but compare the Jade Buddha Temple, completed in 1918 as the resting place for a large jewel-encrusted Buddha brought from Burma a century ago, with temples in Wuhan and elsewhere. It was closed in 1949 and narrowly survived the Cultural Revolution only to be reopened in 1980 and the monks allowed to serve their community once more. Guidebooks sometimes depict it as a tourist come-on, and to some extent that may be true; that photography has recently been permitted inside is one sign of this. But clearly this is also a genuine place of worship. I saw young people, local people, lighting joss sticks and reciting their prayers. Christianity is the religion practised with the least interference — none, as far as I could learn. Mass is once again celebrated at St Ignatius Cathedral, whose spires were truncated during the Cultural Revolution, and there is an American Protestant church, which I was informed has a few parishioners from beyond the small U.S. business community. There were similar signs of a loosened grip in the

Soviet Union. Certainly the Soviets have come a long way from the days when Stalin tore down the Church of Christ the Saviour to put up a building that was to be crowned with a statue of Stalin 30 metres high (the structure proved too heavy for the spongy land and a swimming pool was built on the site instead). The difference is that in the Soviet Union I still would have needed permission from the state religious affairs office to venture very far inside a working church or synagogue, especially if I wanted to talk to a priest or a rabbi. In China I refrained from talking to a Christian cleric for the simple reason that I didn't actually see one, and I didn't want to intrude on any of the Buddhist priests, as the ones I saw always seemed to be at prayer.

Near one religious shrine in Shanghai I saw something that eroded my friend Tian's assertion that in China the size of the fine or penalty for a misdemeanour must always be ominous but nonspecific for the threat to make the people cower. The sign I saw clearly stated that the fine for public expectoration was one yuan. Of course, this was a prohibition that absolutely no one seemed to obey, so maybe he is right after all.

The buzz in Shanghai when I was there was all about politics. The party bosses in Beijing had three concerns. That George Bush, kowtowing to pressure from Congress, might not renew most-favoured-nation status with China. Indeed, this fear extended to the possibility that Bush might damage the economy more not only by cutting down on imports from China but perhaps by causing a big pull-out in the foreign investment that China had been courting with such success right up to the time of Tiananmen. As it was, the Italian partners in one major joint venture in Shanghai had announced their intention to withdraw because business had been so poor since the massacre, only to be told that China couldn't afford to buy them out — a different situation from the one in the U.S.S.R., where foreign partners are frustrated by lack of sophistication in the government and the market and the nonconvertibility of the money.

The second Chinese worry was that the pirate radio ship *Goddess of Democracy*, conceived by exiled pro-democracy students and their sympathizers, would begin its propaganda operations. In the event, America extended China's trading privileges and the radio-ship project had to be abandoned after the U.S., Japan, and Taiwan closed ranks to prevent it from getting the equipment it needed. At a certain level, governments always stick together, sometimes even when they are at war with one another, for war can be a kind of military collaboration against civilians. This trip was not having the slightest effect on my view of socialism one way or another, but I confess that it was adding another layer to my cynicism about government.

Beijing's third fear was of course another outbreak of protest on the June fourth anniversary, and about that one they were more nervous than one might reasonably have expected them to be. With the day in question a week or so away, Jiang Zemin, the party leader, went so far as to say that security forces were being ordered to stop the hunt for students who took part in the movement. I wondered what people like Fang Lizhi and his wife Li Shuxian, who were still in hiding inside the U.S. embassy a year after fleeing there to avoid arrest, thought of that. Soldiers were out in force in Nanjing Road doing public relations duty — shining people's shoes, giving them free haircuts, testing their blood pressure and performing other small public health tasks.

So the place was jittery and reacted excitedly to the news, smuggled in from Hong Kong via Guangzhou, that the senior Beijing official in the Crown colony — Xu Jiatun, head of the New China News Agency there and so a kind of consul-general in waiting — had defected to California. Defection had never been an important part of the cold war in the Pacific the way it was in relations between the western allies and the Eastern bloc, and indeed it wasn't entirely clear whether Xu had truly defected or had taken it on the lam; the story had a sharp effect nonetheless. Suddenly the usual western newspapers were not on display in the hotels patronized by foreigners, and the satellite feed of CNN reverted to snow and static for a minute or two during the world news round-up.

Now I found myself in a tight situation, for the stupidest of reasons.

When I had finally got my journalist's visa from the Chinese consulate in Toronto, I had given the staff there a copy of the itinerary I had already been through with the embassy people in Ottawa, and explained that I would be crossing the border by train at a certain point on such-and-such a day. They professed to understand me, and I foolishly did not bother to check their arithmetic once they returned my passport with the visa stamped inside. A chance look at it now while changing some money showed that I had been travelling for days on a visa that had expired. The consulate still thought I would be flying from Moscow to Beijing and had allowed only one day for the trip. After having so much trouble getting into China, here I was in the ridiculous position of perhaps not being able to get out.

Summoning all his reserves of calm, Wen Dong told me not to worry. These little errors in addition do happen from time to time, he said. But I could see his anxiety growing, and he would disappear at unusual times to return to his hotel room to telephone his superiors in the building on Tiananmen Square. Could they fine me for visa offences? Would they actually detain someone they were clearly hoping to be rid of? At the least I was no doubt prejudicing my future relations with the Chinese, such as the prospects were (though I was hoping most earnestly for a warming in the future — and still am). There was another problem as well. I had to be on a certain Hong Kong flight in order to make a connection to Bangkok, and now the reservation had disappeared from the computer — vanished totally—with what seemed, for a day and a night, to be slight hope of reinstatement. There were no other flights available.

We needed a plan. If some airline didn't come through with a flight out of Shanghai in time, then Wen would throw me on the train to Guangzhou (they were determined to get me to Canton one way or the other!), whence I could take another train to the frontier before it closed at eight-thirty or nine at night and then catch the hovercraft to Hong Kong. That still left the problem of the visa. The answer was to get the Foreign Ministry to spew out some supplemental documents, an extension and a safe passage, and fax them to Shanghai. I gathered from Wen's expression that this was by no means so easy as it sounds, but on the third try the fax arrived. It remained only to be seen, he said, whether the notoriously officious passport officers at Shanghai airport (for by then a seat had opened up) would accept a mere facsimile as being the same as a piece of good paper with red seals and real signatures. To be safe, he called in a government specialist in VIP-handling, who had a security pass for the whole airport and seemed to know all its employees and guards and the latest triumphs and tragedies in their respective families. While I tried to look as innocent as my meagre acting talent would permit, she joked and cajoled us through customs and into the departure lounge for immigration control. Two guards stamped my passport without even looking at it. I thought I was home free.

11

EVIL PERSON GANGS

When I arrived in Bangkok I discovered that the hotel at which I had a reservation did not exist, at least under that name and at that address. Coming as it did at midnight, after a long day of flight delays and customs queues, this was particularly discouraging. Using gestures and what he believed were a few English words, a taxi driver recommended another place, and we took off down back streets and over flimsy bridges, only to pull up at a brightly lit massage parlour several storeys high. I ventured far enough inside to see the teenaged masseuses sitting in a plexiglas room, wearing porcelain number badges on their cocktail dresses. The place was presided over by a formidable, taciturn woman who sat at the till, under twin portraits of the Thai royal family. Seeing my suitcase, she finally stirred herself enough to convey that the hotel I wanted was across the road. I left with the impression that the two businesses enjoyed an interlocking directorate.

The hotel did indeed have a room, and I dragged and pushed myself up to the top floor. There was no lock on the door. I resolved to get some sleep but to find someplace else for my second night in town before departing for Vietnam. When I awoke in the morning there was a gecko on the wall opposite the bed. When these lizards are in a disposition to mate, they puff themselves up like Dizzy Gillespie. But this fellow was perfectly still, trying to act as though I hadn't seen him.

To my intense, almost heart-breaking disappointment I didn't make it inside Vietnam, though I did succeed in getting some fresh information about conditions there. I fear the reader may be losing patience with my tales of bureaucracy, yet I feel I should explain my failure. I shall try to be brief.

I knew of course that Vietnam was something of a shambles economically. That much had been assured by the U.S., which since the end of the war in 1975 has continued to pursue its embargo against the country under the Trading with the Enemy Act of 1917 and other legislation. Only the ubiquitous and oleaginous Ted Turner had somehow managed to carry on business with them. Other nations that might have invested heavily there, such as Japan, have put in some capital but have also joined with Washington in blocking funds for Vietnam from the World Bank and the International Monetary Fund. The U.S. still clings to the pathetically sad notion that there continue to be American PoWs held in the remote jungles. It has also gone on hating Vietnam for following its own example and invading Cambodia, which it did in 1978, putting an end to the four-year bloodbath of the Khmer Rouge but setting off in turn a complex four-way insurgency that only now was showing signs of winding down.

The Vietnamese, nothing if not patient and resilient, have tried to pull themselves up. For example, they have revived their fishing industry, which nearly collapsed in the late 1970s and early 1980s because so many of the fishermen used their boats to flee the country. They have climbed into the number-three ranking in world rice sales, though this is mainly a reflection of the fact that Vietnamese rice is far cheaper than, say, Thai or Chinese rice; it must be so, because it is irregularly shaped, has a nutty taste, and none of the fragrance of the competition's. Each month Vietnam sends two shiploads of rusty metal picked up from the battlefields and gets two shiploads of Indonesian cement in return. Officially, the economy is growing, slightly, but this is a statistical distortion. Unemployment, once unheard of under socialism, is high, some say 30 per cent; income is low, about US$120 per year on average. Everything except some staple foods is scarce; petrol is sold by the bottle. The foreign debt is more than US$13 billion, and one estimate puts the foreign exchange reserves at only $50 million. In 1986, the government announced its own version of *perestroika*, called *doi moi*. What choice did it have? Yet it fears the political agitation that seems inseparable from such restructuring, judging by the very different examples of Eastern Europe, the Soviet Union, and China. Like Cuba, Vietnam sees itself standing alone and has nightmares about a U.S.-backed Contra-style insurgency that will topple the regime and exact revenge for 1975 when the tanks finally came rolling into Saigon from the north. It has gone so far as to accuse its neighbours and near neighbours, from Laos and Cambodia to democratic Thailand, of harbouring CIA-backed guerrilla training bases. Who knows?

Clearly two forces were competing for the vital energies of Vietnam's leaders: anxiety that the government might start to unravel through a combination of external pressures and domestic discontent, and a desperate need to get more foreign cash. I could tell by following the Hong Kong papers that the two were approaching a quiet collision. Officially, this was "Visit Vietnam Year". Tourists were being enticed and even implored to come. But there were few facilities for them, few guides and interpreters or approved places for them to eat. There are only 1,150 hotel rooms in Ho Chi Minh City, compared with 12,000 in Bangkok, 27,000 in Hong Kong or 27,900 in Toronto, three tourist destinations of the same population class. France and Australia, each with very different interests in the region, have put some money into building up the tourist infrastructure, but most investors are reluctant because the economy is so weak. It's a vicious circle. Also, Hanoi has cracked down on individual travellers, for political reasons; the issue is apparently another of the many that still divide the northern and southern parts of the country, to say nothing of the various factions within the government itself. Visit Vietnam Year was further marred, to say the least, when the police began arresting people.

In February, when I was still in Toronto wrestling with the Chinese visa problem, Hanoi started to pick up persons whom it claimed were involved in activities such as distributing subversive literature. Intellectuals and writers and Roman Catholics, both lay and clergy, were the most frequent victims. There were often assertions that the suspects had links to the U.S., Britain, or France. In March, a Politburo member was removed from his post for saying publicly that political liberalism could not come too soon if dissent on the East European scale were to be avoided. The government was especially nervous in April, fearing that the fifteenth anniversary of the fall of Saigon on April 30 would be the excuse for a Tiananmen Square type of demonstration (it wasn't). May held a similar threat in the hundredth anniversary of Ho Chi Minh's birth (which turned out, by all reports, to be a rather pleasant political event — the

Vietnamese don't seem to blame Ho for what has taken place since his death, the way the Russians have begun to blame Lenin and the Chinese, Mao). Yet it is also true that one of the reasons the celebration went smoothly was that so many of the potential troublemakers were locked away. Hanoi admitted arresting fourteen persons in February and March. An exile group based in Paris, the Vietnam Committee on Human Rights, put the number at 6,000 for May alone, bringing the total to 14,600 for a six-month period. Yet if the Vietnam War taught the world nothing else, it taught us never to put much credence in body counts, no matter what the source. As for such dissent as remains, it takes the form of agreement in principle but disagreement about methods, rather like Yeltsin in relation to Gorbachev. The Committee of Resistance is a group of heroes from the war against the Americans who believe that reform should be swifter and more sure; recently, two of the movement's leaders were removed and placed under house arrest, the favoured method of dealing with dangerous people, real or suspected. The Committee of Resistance is linked to the north-south tension whose full extent it is difficult for an outsider to comprehend except to know that it is great. Official sources admit that the Vietnamese army, once the world's third largest but now reduced to fewer than 1 million men, has a serious desertion problem. In one unit, 20 per cent of conscripts have gone over the hill, 34 per cent in another, 50 per cent in still others.

This was the atmosphere in which, while still in Shanghai, I received the alarming news about Michael Morrow, an American journalist during the war who now publishes *Petroleum News*, a trade magazine, in Hong Kong. By coincidence, I had been reading about him only a short while earlier, about how in 1971 he broke the story revealing how Laos was permitting Yao tribespeople trained by the CIA to penetrate as much as 320 kilometres inside

China on espionage missions. I knew little else about him, except that in addition to his publishing activities he did a lot of business consulting in Vietnam and that now, on his twentieth visit there since the war ended, he had been picked up for spying (he was held three weeks). Technically the charge against him, according to both the *Standard* and the *South China Morning Post* in Hong Kong, was that he was found in Danang, a city not named on his visa as one he was cleared to visit. The Vietnamese, I was then forced to presume, must follow the Soviet practice of listing all one's destinations on the visa and checking it at every spot. This prompted me to look at my own, which had been procured by a Vancouver travel agency that was a joint venture with the Vietnamese government. It specified no cities whatever and indeed did not seem to me, on close inspection, to be very official-looking; it was a small form that had been filled in by hand, the mistakes being covered over with correction fluid. I thought I had better make certain that I had the document I needed.

If I had begun the whole trip a few months later I probably could have flown directly from Hong Kong to Ho Chi Minh City on Cathay Pacific. But for the moment, except for a few departures from Indonesia, Malaysia, and the Philippines, the only way into Vietnam was through Bangkok on the twice-weekly flights run by Air Vietnam, the domestic agency, in partnership with Thai Airways. The Vietnamese like to keep control of who is coming in, when.

There is no Vietnamese consular representation in Hong Kong, only a one-person trade mission, and the person in question did not answer the phone. So when I continued on to Bangkok I called Thai Airways, reasoning that, although they had not assisted with my own visa, they must assist with other people's, when dealing with package tours and the like. Besides, as the business partners of Air Vietnam, they might have current information. As a rule, it is only

Thais in the upper-middle-class or higher who can communicate effectively in English, and of course they tend not to be the people found in the service industries. That plus the Thai reluctance to conduct business over the telephone made me hire a *tuk-tuk* and go to the office. Mainly what I learned there was that they were pretty sure that all visitors to Vietnam must arrive and depart via the same airport. This was a blow, as my ticket called for me to enter at Ho Chi Minh and leave from Hanoi (only later did I learn from a report by the Canadian journalist Murray Hiebert in the *Far Eastern Economic Review* that Hanoi had been off-limits to foreign journalists and businesspeople for the past month). My ticket was for the following day. I tried to change it but there seemed nothing I could do. Flights were fully booked for another two weeks and I couldn't count on travelling even then. There was virtually no chance that a wait-listed passenger would get on. In fact, doubly reconfirmed executives and tourists who turn up at an early hour to make certain their names are on the hand-written departure lists are routinely bumped off the flights anyway, after waiting half a day with their tickets in hand; there were accounts of this mess in the newspapers. Visit Vietnam Year indeed.

I tried to call on the Vietnamese embassy in Bangkok, hoping for I don't know what, a kind of low-level miracle, I suppose. The legation is right in Wireless Road, in the heart of embassy row. Less than a block away, guarded by Gurkhas, is the sprawling and impressive British embassy, with its famous statue of Queen Victoria — famous because Thai women consider it the statue of a fertility goddess and make floral offerings to it. The Vietnamese have the most modest mission of the lot, a nondescript pale green building, located, in an irony lost on no one, directly across the street from the rather more formidable U.S. one. The Vietnamese do, however, have the higher flag pole. The old

Viet Cong ensign flutters about the tops of the bottle palms, slapping the face of Uncle Sam every time the wind blows. The phone was not working (a common complaint in Bangkok), and when I did get through I exhausted five staff members in turn, trying to explain my problem, first in English and then in the Diefenbakerish French that is the strongest cultural bond between the Vietnamese and the people of English Canada. All I knew at the conclusion was that I needed a Mr Dhan or perhaps Dhang and that he wasn't in. Owing to the unrelieved traffic congestion, movement in Bangkok is slow to difficult. A German entrepreneur had told me at breakfast that he could do only two or at most two and a half brief appointments per day, owing to the tie-ups. When I got to the embassy it was siesta time. When I returned later, Mr Dhan had not reappeared and was expected only vaguely at some point in the future. The flight left without me.

But failure releases its own type of adrenalin, and I was determined to make the best of the situation. I was in Bangkok after all, which even during the war years was the primary listening-post for Vietnam, not least because it has a fairly large Vietnamese community going back to the days of the French-Indochina war in the mid-1940s. Now that it was the only real means of access and egress, it was even more full of Vietnam-watchers than it had been for years, including the hustlers and promoters sniffing about for something to buy or sell and the staffs at the fifty embassies in the city. What's more, my *Whig* colleague David Warren had kindly provided me with a letter of introduction to surviving cronies from his days at the *Bangkok Post*. I would set up a hectic schedule of buying drinks for people and see what I could learn, using the nights, when it was somewhat cooler, to write up these notes of the trip to date.

What I found out is what I have set down so far, but with an abundance of other detail and a bit more context. The whole region is changing quite as much as Europe is, with some developments almost as abrupt. While I was in Bangkok, for example, Myanmar, formerly Burma, which has been more or less forbidden territory to foreigners since the end of the Second World War, locked in its own complex internal struggle, held its first election in thirty years. It seems to have been a surprisingly fair one at that, though the losers (the military, who clamped down on a democracy movement in 1988) appear determined not to vacate the palace without a fight. The possibility of peace in Cambodia holds out even more promise, not least because it would help end Vietnam's diplomatic isolation, particularly from China. That would affect Vietnam's potential for foreign investment; without China, and given the Americans' continued refusal to make up to the people whose country they devastated, the Taiwanese and the South Koreans would likely be the big players. Such news was another sign, as though another were needed, that a new Asia has emerged without the sort of reference to the West that had existed in the era whose artefacts I had been seeking out with an antiquary's interest: an Asia as cautious as it is monolithic.

Not that the West isn't persistent in Asia. For example, the British bank Standard Chartered, which began doing business in Saigon in the 1870s, then opened its own branch in 1904 and managed to hang on until 1977, through three wars and two years of communist rule, is moving back. In fact, for various reasons, most of them global rather than regional, English is replacing French as the second language of Vietnam. This is at least one of the pieces of news that has rankled the French, who see their old cultural stake in Vietnam, Laos, and Cambodia as inseparable from any revival, on a small scale, of their commercial interests there. "When you get to Vietnam," someone told me — I now take that to mean when I do succeed in getting there eventually, I hope sooner rather than later — "you will find French businessmen in your hotel. Most of them *are* French businessmen." The suggestion was that the others would be from the Direction Général de la Sécurité Extérieure or some similar agency. Two diplomats told me that Canada is in an enviable position to invest in Vietnam should relations between the two countries be re-established anytime soon, in view of the special trust that attaches to Canada's being French as well as English. But they felt that Canada would probably miss its chance out of deference to Washington.

Vietnam will have to change substantially, and very quickly, if it is to join the game. It will either have to accept repatriated boat people in a better political and economic environment than the one they fled or else open the gate for unrestrained exodus, but that is too complicated an issue to go into here.

No doubt I had failed to get into Vietnam by being too prudent (that will teach me), but it certainly seemed as though the Vietnamese didn't want me and that had I got in I would have had trouble getting out if for no other reason than that the authorities there, in their uncertainty, kept changing the rules every day. The Soviets didn't want me, the Chinese didn't want me, the Vietnamese didn't want me either. A less insensitive person than myself might have begun to notice a pattern. But me, I was merely glum with immediate disappointment, and in that condition I found Bangkok a less than attractive place to be. I went there hoping, for instance, to see a performance of the ancient *lakhon ling*, or ceremonial monkey theatre. What I saw instead, in a smart shopping street in Bangkok, was a woman with a poor dog she had dyed bright yellow.

The Thais have done a fine public relations job on the rest of the world. Their advertising slogan is "Land of

Smiles", and the visitor is bombarded with the image of happy people saying *sawasdee* in greeting or farewell as they bring their palms together in a prayer-like gesture and give a little bow. I learned nothing of the countryside; I had planned one day to travel up to Chiang Mai in the north but stopped in disgust when I read in the *Nation* that morning that the American FBI was there that week, running one of its National Academy in Asia programmes designed to bring Thai police up to date on interrogation techniques. But speaking only of Bangkok, I found, in my blue mood, that being there was like being locked in a sauna with fifteen heroin addicts who have really poor taste in music.

Tourists are somehow led to believe that the city is as ancient as the authentic Thai culture, which began to form when the Khmer civilization was driven out some 800 years ago. In fact, Bangkok was decreed into being in the late eighteenth century because its defensive position on the Chao Phraya River made it a difficult target for the Burmese (who had already invaded twice, on battle elephants, and been expelled) or the Vietnamese or the Laos. The place was meant to recapture the glories of Ayuthaya, which had been destroyed after serving as the administrative centre for four centuries. Ayuthaya had been quite a town; it had 400 *wats* or temples; as early as the seventeenth century there were 47 kilometres of paved streets there. Bangkok (*bang kok*, village of the plum-olive trees) was a poor substitute, despite a system of canals, which are now either filled in or stagnant.

I had the poor luck to be there just as the hot season was giving way to the rainy season. Not that the one had been replaced by the other; the two kinds of discomfort coexist. You had only to step outside early in the morning to be bent down by the heat, which has the force and effect of gravity. But at the stroke of noon a curtain of rain would descend and remain until 11 p.m. precisely. It is a punctual, work-to-rule kind of rain. Once a year the river spills its banks and inundates the city to a depth of a metre or more. The floods are a little worse each time because Bangkok, like Shanghai, is built on ooze and is steadily sinking — in Bangkok's case, by 12.5 centimetres per annum. As for the matter of canals, what's charming in Venice or Leningrad is otherwise in Bangkok.

Thailand managed to escape colonization by the British, Dutch, or French, but sided with the Japanese in the Second World War and so briefly became a colonial power itself when it was given Laos and Cambodia as an immediate reward (but was forced to return them in 1945). Then it came into the American orbit. After a series of coups and counter-coups, the most recent in 1981, it remains what it has been for so long, a constitutional monarchy that is actually run by the military. Still, the country is far less authoritarian than Singapore, and apparently quite stable as well, despite having had eleven constitutions since 1932. Thais are also the world's most vocal monarchists. They are serious about their Buddhism as well, though devotion varies according to generation and locality. Most people practise Hinayana Buddhism, except for the Vietnamese and the residents of Chinatown, who are Mahayana Buddhists; there are also 2 million Sunni Muslims, mostly in the south, and a couple of hundred thousand Shi'ites. Bangkok, where monks often have their photographs taken blessing new places of business, has a lot of *wats* for the tourists. While I was there I was struck by a press report from Phuket province of a monk addicted to heroin, the local cash crop, who beat a brother monk to death inside their temple with a wooden pole; the motive was robbery. Section 206, subsections 2 and 7 of the Criminal Code make it an offence "To use the lower part of the body to point to a statue of Buddha, pagoda, stupa, mosque or cross" and "To put a statue of Buddha, or the head of such a statue, in a wardrobe together with men's or women's clothing."

Of all the world's peoples, perhaps only the Americans are more patriotic than the Thais. Like many others before me, I have often observed that this emotion is sometimes found in conditions that are favourable to the cultivation of hypocrisy, and I couldn't help but notice that movies shown on cable television are censored, clumsily and heavily, to remove the slightest reference to sex. I speak not of what American call X- or even PG-rated movies but of routine inoffensive Hollywood films. "The censors", I was told, "apparently have an interest in the video stores, all of which have uncensored films for hire in the back rooms. Everyone here is on the fiddle, you see." Notwithstanding that perfectly logical explanation, I found such censorship, and Thai prudery in general, somewhat curious in a place where sleazy sex is one of the biggest industries, employing, if that is the right word, up to 1 million Thai women, or one in every fifty-five citizens, and bringing in uncounted wealth in foreign exchange.

Everybody knows about Patpong, the sex district — actually Patpongs I and II, a couple of parallel streets, now augmented by such others as Soi Cowboy off Sukhumvit near Soi 21. Defenders like to suggest that this represents the continuation of a tradition with roots in ancient Thai culture. In fact, Thailand's first massage parlour opened only in 1956, offering the sort of legitimate "traditional" or "Thai" massage once administered by masseuses outside *wats*. The place had a mainly Japanese clientele and was soon driven out of business by "massage" parlours. Bangkok was the closest and least expensive of the R&R destinations for American servicemen in Vietnam, and it is widely supposed that it was they who remade the face of Patpong, as they did Kings Cross in Sydney. "But in the days before the Vietnam buildup," writes Alan Dawson, a

Canadian journalist who was given U.S. citizenship for fighting on the American side, "Patpong was without doubt a respectable street, although a drink was available." Girlie bars didn't begin concentrating there until the 1970s. But it is easy to see how the misconception began, given that the dominant type of performing was and remains what was called (I write this for the benefit of Young People) go-go dancing. Sex-for-hire as an economic staple came slightly later. Live sex acts on stage as a form of theatre arrived only in the mid-1980s; the first establishment to make a specialty of them was owned by a former police officer. Yet if it is not literally correct to say that the Vietnam War made Patpong what it is today, it is surely true to say that the Vietnam War aesthetic still flourishes there — after a rough couple of months killing Buddhist rice farmers, what better relaxation than enslaving young Thai girls from the countryside (the legal age is thirteen and the slavery is disguised by contract)? The sex shows are nothing that a grown man hasn't seen before without any benefit whatsoever and that women would wish to see even less — prostitutes shooting darts at a balloon using only their vaginal muscles, for example. As for actual sex, all other considerations aside, a person would have to be suicidal to buy any in Bangkok. AIDS is a touchy subject, related as it is to the balance of payments, but various estimates put the rate of HIV infection among massage personnel at between 50 and 80 per cent, rising as one goes further down on the price scale, which tracks the educational curve. The newspapers accept advertisements for hererosexual sex only, but to judge from the abundant promotional matter of other types, perhaps half of the sex-for-sale is gay sex, and this no doubt has some influence on the AIDS problem.

The area is not without its crime problem as well. I copied the following from a handbook of advice for visitors. It was written by a local solicitor whose knowledge of English is less advanced than his practical counsel:

> I have known some message from a newspaper that there are evil person gangs act in a manner likely giving well-intentioned advice by volunteer to keep a credit card of tourist by using any means of fraud until a tourist approves. And then the evil person gangs will take the credit card to change money wonderfully that the tourists has not known about this. The tourist has known that not money in his credit card when he has come back to his house. Then it is too late. So you should keep your credit card with yourself all the time.

Bangkok has whorehouses that are also coffee shops and whorehouses that are also barbering salons. It does not, so far as anyone told me, have a combination whorehouse-stock exchange, but that would be the perfect expression of Thai society in the 1990s. Under a government and a military so conservative that a core of powerful people persist in prepping mentally for a Vietnamese invasion, Thailand has longed to practise slash-and-burn capitalism. With commodity prices up, manufacturing coming abreast of agriculture, and exports bounding, there is money in the air. In 1989, the U.S. economy grew by 2.9 per cent, the Japanese by 4.8 per cent, and the Thai by 11 per cent. But the price of profit is high. The country's attitude towards the environment has always been casual, and now air, water, and land pollution are becoming alarming; I saw a few people in Bangkok wearing face masks, in the Japanese manner. There is virtually no urban planning or even zoning, and the construction boom is rapidly depriving Bangkok of whatever charm or even order it once had. There are over 30 million people in the country's labour force (70 per cent of them still in agriculture), but that figure takes into account ones as young as eleven. Many workers first have to buy their jobs from employers for cash. But every month, 4,000 Thai technicians, some of the best-trained individuals in the labour pool, leave for contract positions in Saudi Arabia — or did, until the Iraqi occupation of Kuwait. This outflow was halted at one point after three Saudi diplomats were assaulted in Bangkok and in retaliation the Saudis stopped giving out work visas; at the time of the Kuwait invasion, which changed the whole picture in the Middle East, there were believed to be 150,000 Thais working for the Saudis.

Like the Soviet Union, like China, like Vietnam, Thailand is undergoing a kind of revolution or counter-revolution or whatever you wish to call it. Like the Soviet one in particular, it has less to do with ideology than with necessity, but the aim is similar in all these cases: to create a middle class where there was none before. Hong Kong is different. It has a middle class but is having difficulty holding on to it.

Five hundred resident Canadians in Thailand are registered with the Canadian embassy in Bangkok, which is one of the Fort Zinderneufs of the external affairs department; there are probably as many again who have not checked in. But fully 100,000 Canadian tourists go to Thailand every year, a threefold increase since 1985. By comparison, there are only 200,000 U.S. visitors in Thailand annually, an indication that a decade and a half after the late unpleasantness in Vietnam, the Americans are still skittish about Southeast Asia. Hong Kong, though, has 30,000 Canadian expatriates, and the Canadian commission there is by far the busiest post in our diplomatic system insofar as visa applications are concerned. The reason of course is that so many Hongkongese are attempting to get into Canada.

At this writing about 600 per week are boarding what people there call the Maple Leaf Express, and the number is climbing quickly. Some upper-middle- and upper-class Hong

Kong people have begun to send their friends emigration cards. These are similar to change-of-address cards and often conclude with the sentiment, "We look forward to seeing you in Canada." One Hong Kong newspaper columnist has observed that when a person idly asks an expectant mother where she intends to have her baby, the woman answers not by specifying a hospital but a country — Hong Kong or Canada. This atmosphere is reflected in ways both subtle and obvious. Suddenly *The Globe and Mail* is easy to find in Hong Kong. And whereas Canadian furs are all but banned from the marketplace in Europe, they are very popular in stiflingly hot Hong Kong, as long as the shop has *Canada* in its name and the goods are expensive.

Education is another field where Canadianism is a fashionable necessity. "School here is a business", Margaret Greer, twenty-eight, told me. "Only 30 per cent of students attend the fully funded government schools." The rest go to privately funded ones like Delia School of Canada, where both she and her husband, Garry, thirty-eight, taught for almost two years before returning recently to their home in Kingston. The oldest, most exclusive private schools in the colony, such as the King George V School, locally known as KG5, are still the most desirable, but lately there has been a boomlet in schools that have accreditation from one or more Canadian provinces and thus promise the graduate easy passage to some Canadian university. The Delia School has about 525 primary and secondary students learning the Ontario and the Nova Scotia curricula respectively. The Canadian Overseas School, across the harbour on the Kowloon side, offers the Ontario curriculum exclusively; a school opened in autumn 1990 offers the Manitoba programme. Not since Expo and the Centennial has Canadian culture been so popular anywhere outside Canada, but this time the reasons are different. Not admiration but panic, not respect but curiosity and fear of the future.

Hong Kong exists, at least in its present form, as a British Crown colony of immense sophistication and enormous wealth, as a result of the biggest drug deal in history, and now the deal is turning sour, almost a century after it went down. In the Convention of Chuen Pee at the conclusion of the opium war of 1841, China was compelled to cede Hong Kong Island to the British in perpetuity. In 1860, the tip of the Kowloon Peninsula and a dollop of land called Stonecutters Island were also signed away forever. But in 1898, in the Second Treaty of Peking, the British didn't press so hard to get freehold; the 588 square-kilometre area called the New Territories was leased for only ninety-nine years, like a London townhouse. As the last few precious years drain away, people grow uneasy, then worse than uneasy. The negotiation that began in 1982 and concluded in 1984 about how the People's Republic would take over and manage the colony was little comfort. After the slaughter in Tiananmen Square and the ongoing repression that followed, whatever hope there was turned to dread, even terror. For here is the idiotic irony of it all: the only time the world had any need of Margaret Thatcher's bloody-mindedness, she turned out to be a wimp. Why didn't she take the view that the Chinese abrogated the deal by their actions against the students in Beijing? Why didn't she consider what repression or worse could accompany the arrival of the People's Liberation Army in Hong Kong? Why, in short, didn't the Iron Lady, who went to war to protect British sheep on the Falklands, close the border with China? The answer is that the sheep were white.

 The deliberate shows of confidence in Hong Kong that were underway before the massacre have been carried forward (though when I was there, Hong Kong came to realize that Donald Trump, given his financial reverses in New York, would not build a Trump Tower in the colony, as he had planned). Certainly many locals, as well as the British, continue to invest and breed, attracted, to no one can say what extent, by gambler's daring and the smell of a bargain. Yet such activity seems to be so much whistling past the graveyard. On closer examination, the rats, such as Rupert Murdoch, who has sold his half-interest in the *South China Morning Post*, are deserting, or at least making contingency plans, and the most conspicuous new building in Hong Kong, and perhaps its most conspicuous manmade landmark, is the tower of the state bank of the PRC, the Bank of China. Beijing has also announced its intention of helping to build the new airport that was to have stabilized confidence and been a symbol of the continuity of capital.

What all this means for Hong Kong citizens is that those who can secure a foreign passport are doing so. One New Canadian in six is from Hong Kong. To stem the flow into Britain, the government, after a lengthy debate, has reluctantly announced that it will grant U.K. passports to 50,000 administrations and officials in the colony — about 250,000 people in all, when family members are included. The plan was that, by dispensing such peace of mind, London would be permitting the colony to run smoothly for the next several years, because the key personnel would know that they had a place to go after the change-over; but Beijing has seen this merely as a way to ensure British influence into the new century. Meanwhile, at the level of individual souls, the desperation becomes more apparent. People whose whole lives are rooted in the concept of the family have shut up aged parents in nursing homes and disowned children with handicaps so that nothing will impede their desirability as immigrants to Canada or some other place. Dead relatives are less of a problem: cremation, which took place in only 50 per cent of cases a decade ago, has climbed to 90 per cent, as Chinese emigrants now take their ancestors with them. The love and enjoyment of wealth, with which Hong Kong has been associated for so long, seem now to be giving way to a deeper greed, as people attempt to make as much money as they can as quickly as they can, in preparation for a rainy day — the skies are darkening already.

I found three sets of public service ads running on television one evening. The first urged citizens to turn in members of the triads who might try to extort money or do violence against them. The second pleaded with gang members to turn themselves in (which they are all the more reluctant to do because it has long been understood that organized crime infiltrates the Royal Hongkong Police). The third advertisement was for more police recruits.

There is an in-migration to counterbalance but by no means cancel out the out-migration: the Vietnamese boat people who started coming in 1978 and continue to arrive even now. The pace of reform in Vietnam remains such that Hong Kong, for all its problems, looks pretty attractive. The thought of Hong Kong under Chinese rule is of course less terrifying to the Vietnamese than it is to even the smallest of Hong Kong capitalists, not only the silk-suited young men with their cellular phones who make deals on street corners but even those sampan-dwellers with their pocket scales for weighing small quantities of fish and rice.

Hong Kong has been inundated with refugees before, after the collapse of the Qing dynasty in 1911, after Shanghai fell first to the Japanese in 1937 and then to the communists in 1950. However dislocating those movements were, they also benefited Hong Kong by remaking it, reinvigorating it. The colony's history as a textile centre, for example, may be attributed to Mao Zedong. But this time the situation is different. The arrivals are locked up until they can be sent back home.

The profile of the boat people is changing, and various authorities profess to find good news in the shifting statistics. When the western media began repeating the horror stories about Thai pirates who prey on boat people, the government in Bangkok responded by setting up a commission for the suppression of piracy, which now claims to show that its efforts have cleaned up the sea lanes. In fact, the number of reported incidents — of the small percentage actually reported — has declined because most of the refugees now are in fact ethnic Chinese from southern Vietnam who can smuggle themselves across the border into the People's Republic and only then use a boat, to descend the Pearl River to Hong Kong, where some 90 per cent of them are turned away on the grounds that they are merely economic migrants, not refugees. The others are sent to detention camps to await enforced repatriation. In May 1990, when I was there, 800 boat people still made it to Hong Kong, compared with 9,000 in the same month one year earlier. At the same time, the police made a sweep of one camp, Whitehead, acting in response to stories of gang violence inside, and took away 180 people, some of them minors, and then made the rounds of the other camps scattered in secluded spots round the territory while a special facility was set aside for troublemakers. The camps are overseen by the United Nations High Commission for Refugees, but the agency is quickly running out of money.

My last day before returning to Canada I talked my way into one of the camps — Bowring, in the Tuen Mun District. It is only one-fifth the size of Whitehead but houses about 1,000 men and women (average age thirty-five) and an equal number of children. They are crowded into Nissen huts formerly used for British troops and now fitted out as crude dormitories, the tiers of bunks separated by blankets. The air was heavy with the smell of cooking fish and the odour of too many bodies in too small a space. The light was poor, and people's laundry hung everywhere. There is a school and a small library within the compound. Atop a tiny hill, isolated from the other buildings, is L Block, a brick building divided up into ten airless cells, each about

1.5 by 2.5 metres. This is where the problem cases are kept. Problem cases are defined as those caught stealing or fighting or abusing women. A week earlier, Hong Kong police made one of their surprise inspections at seven in the morning and confiscated a quantity of homemade weapons, yet the owners of them weren't put in the cells. The people at Bowring are Vietnamese rather than ethnic Chinese, and they are all from the north. Those from the south and those from the north must be kept in separate camps lest they kill each other; perhaps this is the most telling of all indications of what Vietnam must be like fifteen years after Reunification.

"This is an open centre", William Lau, the head of Bowring, explained to me as we tramped around the compound, with small children darting around us but the adults keeping their distance, pretending to be busy and otherwise avoiding eye contact with us. "This means that under the reforms that came into effect last month, the people here are free to find jobs on the outside and return at night." They leave their identification with the guards when they go out and retrieve it when they come back in the evening. These are all legitimate refugees fleeing persecution, the others having been screened out and made to wait to be returned. They will be here "a year or two" before they move on to a third country, assuming they have relatives to sponsor them in Canada, the U.S., Australia, or elsewhere. By 1997, it is expected there will be a build-up of as many as 30,000 people who cannot return but were rejected for life elsewhere. Current plans call for the British simply to leave them for the Chinese to worry about.

Lau told me, "We have many voluntary agencies involved here, and Hong Kong people run a job placement bureau." The most common jobs are as labourers. "Sanitation is a big worry. Health care is generally better. We have an English nurse." A sort of prisoners' committee meets every

Evil Person Gangs

Wednesday morning to work out complaints and resolve difficulties with Lau and his staff, who spend some of their time arranging for donations of food. Someone recently gave one tonne of candy, which just before I arrived had been made up into individual bags.

After the tour we repaired to Lau's office, where I saw the results of the morning's roll call written on a chalk board: "In camp, 2050. Missing, 157. Detained by police, 1." He asked me where I was from and when I told him he replied, "Ah, yes, Kingston in Canada, a beautiful spot. I have taken a boat tour of the Thousand Islands."

I expressed surprise that he had been there. He answered that he knew Ontario well, because his brother now works for IBM in Toronto, their parents have moved to Don Mills, and he is hopeful — though he hadn't heard the decision yet — that his daughter might be accepted at the University of Toronto.

As I was leaving he said to me, "Perhaps you and I shall meet again one day when my work here is done." He was not being sly or ironic.

"Maybe so", I replied. "That would be pleasant."

We shook hands and he walked me to the checkpoint where there was a gate in the barbed-wire fence. Two English guards were cracking jokes on the other side.